THE LAST HUMANITY

ALSO AVAILABLE FROM BLOOMSBURY

Clandestine Theology: A Non-Philosopher's Confession of Faith, François Laruelle

Philosophies of Difference: A Critical Introduction to Non-Philosophy, François Laruelle

Anti-Badiou: The Introduction of Maoism into Philosophy, François Laruelle

Principles of Non-Philosophy, François Laruelle

THE LAST HUMANITY

The New Ecological Science

FRANÇOIS LARUELLE

TRANSLATED BY ANTHONY PAUL SMITH

BLOOMSBURY ACADEMIC
LONDON • NEW YORK • OXFORD • NEW DELHI • SYDNEY

BLOOMSBURY ACADEMIC
Bloomsbury Publishing Plc
50 Bedford Square, London, WC1B 3DP, UK
1385 Broadway, New York, NY 10018, USA

BLOOMSBURY, BLOOMSBURY ACADEMIC and the Diana logo are trademarks
of Bloomsbury Publishing Plc

First published in 2015 in France as 'En dernière humanité' by François Laruelle
© Éditions du Cerf

First published in Great Britain 2021

Cover image: Mike Kelley, 2007-08 (digital projection, 8-minute loop),
(© Jennifer Steinkamp / Museum of Fine Arts, Houston, Texas, USA / Bridgeman Images)

A catalogue record for this book is available from the British Library.

A catalog record for this book is available from the Library of Congress.

ISBN: HB: 978-1-3500-0822-9
        PB: 978-1-3500-0823-6
        ePDF: 978-1-3500-0821-2
        eBook: 978-1-3500-0824-3

Typeset by RefineCatch Limited, Bungay, Suffolk

To find out more about our authors and books visit www.bloomsbury.com
and sign up for our newsletters.

CONTENTS

TRANSLATOR'S INTRODUCTION: WHY ECOLOGY AT THE END?

ANTHONY PAUL SMITH

The generation coming to be today may be the last of humanity. The grand apocalyptic visions of religion have not come to pass, but have instead given way to prosaic litanies of violence, suffering, death, and extinction reported in the news and shared on social media alongside banal details about reality stars and the day-to-day fluctuations of the global market. Who would have thought the end of the world would be so dull, that the death of species would go so unnoticed? Throughout the world, the various and uneven struggles for survival require so much energy, so much attention, that the struggles of others pass without being seen. Whether what is lived be human, animal, or plant, they all pass into the rushing flux of a generalized death, a generalized extinction, a shared fate that we may call ecological.

This is the background against which thinking—be it philosophical or not—finds itself being practiced today. The climate crisis is what pushes ecology as a way of thinking to the fore of human consciousness. For it is certain ecological theories and the results of certain ecological researches that has brought global humanity face to face with the material and natural basis of our existence, with the horror of interconnectedness that links all living and dead things (as well as links these to the never-living). Horror because nothing we do appears to escape ecological reality and while it may be true that nothing we do escapes mathematical reality either, the nature of ecological reality is the nature of bodies, of flesh, of eating, of fucking, of shitting, of leaking bodily fluids, of gases, and of dying. That is, the science of ecology brings us face to face with what is abject, with what is visceral, in ways that more seemingly abstract sciences cannot and in ways that other biological sciences are unable to do in regard to the overwhelming immensity of connection.

François Laruelle's project of non-philosophy or non-standard philosophy rarely touches in a direct way on contemporary problems. Laruelle himself does not intervene in public debates about this political policy or that social problem in the way that many of his contemporaries have. In an extended interview with the journalist and trained philosopher Philippe Petit, Laruelle is indeed invited to pronounce on various issues of the day and steadfastly refuses. While he acknowledges that, "of course as an ordinary citizen I have 'my opinions'," his discussion remains at the level of abstraction, at the level of the generic.[1] *The Last Humanity*, even though it emerges out of the conditions for thought given by the climate crisis and so represents his most direct engagement with a live political and social problem, continues this practice of focusing on the work of abstraction, of thinking. In this introduction I will not be translating what Laruelle has said about ecology into some simpler form. The work of translation has already taken place and what Laruelle has written is what he has written. Instead, this introduction will contextualize Laruelle's engagement with ecology by considering what ecology as a name refers to, why the project of non-philosophy has now engaged with this ecology, and possible paths of research that this engagement makes visible, possibly especially for those who may be the last humanity.

Ecology Is Said in Many Ways

In *The Last Humanity* Laruelle tells his readers that ecology has come to rival philosophy. We will explore why he says this a little later, but first it is important to understand what exactly ecology names in this rivalry. While Laruelle does not explicitly state this, it is very clear from his description early on in the text that he is not referring to the purely scientific theory and practice that goes under the name of ecology, but to a more expansive way of thinking and sensibility toward experience.

The science of ecology is generally considered to be a new science, coming to be distinct in the 18th century and even then, only in the mid-20th century gaining prominence. The use of the term ecology in the sense still carried today is usually attributed to the German zoologist Ernst Haeckel whose coinage of the German word *Ökologie* borrowed from the Greek words *oikos* or "household" and *logos*, which usually translates to "science" but also "logic" and "word" or "speech". Early ecological theory attempted to explain the interconnected nature of life in the light of Darwin's discoveries concerning the evolution of species in relation to one another and their shared environment. The history of ecology and its contemporary principles as a science are not well known or understood in our general culture and when people talk about this or that practice being "ecological" they tend to mean something more general about the relationship between humanity and non-human nature, between how we live and the effects it has on the wider ecological system we are a part of. These ideas are derived from ecological science, but largely without a strong understanding of their scientific source, the conceptual meaning, or the debates and different approaches and scales found in scientific ecology.

Some theorists, including those within the natural and social sciences as well as the humanities, distinguish between "political ecology" and the purely scientific field of ecology. Political ecology in this case refers to the sense that ecology has an obvious bearing on certain social and political questions and should be used as a management tool within the political and social field. One such theorist, the French ecologist Christian Lévêque, notes that many people belie the distinctions between political ecology and scientific ecology and with good reason as the science of ecology does clearly impact the social and political lives of human beings.[2] Lévêque, like other ecologists, thinks it is important to maintain the distinction, to allow for ecology to be a science of knowledge and to not be a mere political tool of management. Yet, such a distinction is increasingly difficult to maintain and it is a live debate over whether or not such a distinction is desirable.

Ecology in everyday discourse tends to be associated with justice movements, be they social justice for human beings, calling for greater animal rights, or justice for the land itself. Such associations may lead many to assume that the history of both scientific and political ecology is a history of progressive justice. A popular example of ecology's link to a progressive justice ethic is found in one of the most important works of contemporary ecological ethics entitled "The Land Ethic," written by the prominent ecologist Aldo Leopold in 1949. There Leopold argues that a "land ethic," which deals with the relationship between human society and the wider environment, is a probable and ecologically necessary part of an "ethical sequence." This sequence moves from the relation of two individuals to the individual's relation to society and then calls for the as yet undeveloped land ethic.[3] Leopold explains that as part of the ethical sequence, "The land ethic simply enlarges the boundaries of the community to include soils, waters, plants, and animals, or collectively: the land."[4]

Here we see an early ecological version of what Laruelle refers to as the Man, Animal, Plant system or simply "MAP" explicitly linked to ethics. In line with Laruelle's own characterization of the MAP system, this vision of ecology occludes the question of how such boundaries are set and the ways in which communities are created through the exclusion of strangers who are not part of that community. The belief that ecology is aligned with social justice in some essential way is only possible because of the general ignorance of the history of ecology where ecology as a science has been part of the colonial division of the world into colonizer and colonized, of those who are part of the community, inclusive of the land, and those who are not. Indeed, though Leopold has a rather prosaic sense of the ethical sequence, he is writing prior to even the modest reforms of the US Civil Rights movement or the victories of anti-colonial struggles elsewhere and appears to be oblivious to the interrelated nature of the land and the racist divisions imposed upon humanity.

When Lévêque bemoans the collapse of distinction between scientific and political ecology he is not only referring to the ways in which scientific ecology as a science of knowledge is put to use for liberal or left-wing politics, as many would assume today. Rather, the political use of ecology begins with attempts at the "scientific management" of ecosystems in lands that have been colonized by Europeans.[5] Even the concept that is arguably primary within ecology today, the ecosystem concept, arose within a colonial episteme as a debate between various figures involved in empire building and management. Alfred George Tansley, a British ecologist, introduced the term "ecosystem" in his 1935 polemical article "The Use and Abuse of Vegetational Concepts and Terms". His initial conception of the ecosystem helped clear away the philosophical debates between materialists and idealists that had determined the scientific study of ecology up to that point in their framing of the interpretation of scientific data. The subject of Tansley's criticism was the white South African ecologist John Phillips who in a series of four articles had attempted to defend a version of philosophical holism for ecology. This holism was behind a vulgar form of vitalism that held sway in ecology through the work of the American Fredric Clements and Jan Christian Smuts who was a white South African scientist, military general, prime minister, and early advocate of apartheid.[6] In other words, at the birth of this vital ecological concept we see a need to short-circuit philosophical debates that were taking place among ecologists—an early form of the rivalry identified by Laruelle—but, as with Leopold's land ethic, without any sense of the ways in which ecology as a science was still engaged in the colonial episteme.

Ecology and Non-Philosophy

Ecology is thus said in many ways, indeed many more ways than the short sketch above can even gesture at. This does not mean, however, that there is no coherent use of the term ecology. Just as Laruelle argues regarding the differences within philosophy still manifest around a central identity and practice, ecology names a particular kind of thinking and practice. When Laruelle uses the term ecology he appears not to belie this difference, but to name the two things together. Ecology is both a science of knowledge (for Laruelle specifically a knowledge about life) and a discourse about the ways in which human beings should live among each other and in the wider environment.[7]

At times his use of the name ecology is positive, for instance saying that it is the greater thought that comes after philosophy paralleling Nietzsche's Zarathustra speaking of the greater overman that comes after man. At other times Laruelle's use is negative, modifying ecology with the descriptors "vulgar and cynical." In being both, ecology has come to name a massive, overwhelmingly determinative form of thinking and practice as well as to name its more distinctive and potentially disruptive and insurrectionary aspects. It is not simply that ecology, as such an over-determining mode of thought, is to be rejected, but that its form signifies that it shares much in common with other over-determining forms of thought, like philosophy and theology. Those projects are real human attempts to understand and modify reality, or more precisely "the Real" in Laruelle's terminology, which is always foreclosed from our thought and unable to be captured by the very thought that is radically immanent (to) itself.[8] Yet, these attempts also fail in so far as they come to decide upon the identity of the human, of the Real itself, as well as the differential identity of the animal and the plant. These identities, which form the MAP system as

Laruelle understands ecology to be concerned with (of course this says nothing about the decision regarding biosphere, ecosystem, biome, or even nature and a number of other important aspects of ecological science that are elided here), come to confuse these identities with the Real itself, with the what is in-the-last-humanity itself. In other words, these discourses come to have faith in their own circularity, to see their own act of decision as the Real itself, instead of remaining perpetually open and in a movement of thought. This can come to have violent effects and has indeed done so historically in the ways that ecology and colonialism have been wrapped up with one another.

The project of non-philosophy is, in part, an attempt to undo or mitigate the violent effects of philosophy. As Laruelle comments in an interview, "Non-philosophy, I would say, is a weapon of last defence [*défense ultime*] because I think that philosophy, left to its spontaneous presuppositions, is not very favorable to man."[9] As a massive, over-determining form of thought this ecology carries with it this shared trait with philosophy. We have gestured toward the history of violence present in ecological thinking, but it is important to see that this shared trait with philosophy (and theology before it) is partly what calls for a non-philosophical engagement with ecology. One thing that is interesting about ecology as described by Laruelle is its closeness to certain elements of non-philosophy. It would be difficult for readers of Laruelle's other works not to see that closeness when he writes in this book, "Ecology is not an ontological object, it is a reform of philosophy by a new science." Ecology in the general sense he employs the term as a rival to philosophy, names a kind of unified theory of elements of philosophy (ethics and identity, among others) with a scientific posture. This mirrors the way that Laruelle presents non-philosophy, especially in major works like *Philosophy and Non-Philosophy* and *Principles of Non-Philosophy*.

In recognizing the need for ecology to undergo a non-philosophical critique, Laruelle is not seeking to undermine or destroy ecology or to stop its overtaking of philosophy any more than his own critical refinement of non-philosophy itself is an attempt to destroy that project. Instead, there is a recognition here that attempts to disempower philosophy's violence, attempts which include non-philosophy and ecology, must face the ways such violence can be repeated in the very attempt to undo violence, the ways in which authority can be created in the undoing of authority.[10]

Another End of the World Is Possible

In its scientific and political forms ecology has, like philosophy, been in the business of defining "Man" through distinctions and differential relations to the animal and the plant. I have elsewhere registered my disagreement with Laruelle's use of the French term *homme* or "man" as the generic term for the species-being of humanity. Throughout my translations of his work I have tried to undercut, when appropriate, this heteronormative gendering that undermines the generic task of non-philosophy.[11] Yet, in this instance, it does allow us for a potentially fruitful interaction with the radical work of others like Sylvia Wynter who has traced the ways religion, philosophy, and science have been marshaled to create the "overrepresentation" of the human as "Man."[12]

Wynter's work is concerned in part with the way that the creation of race is part of the overrepresentation of the human by "Man." Ecology, like other biological sciences that arise out of a colonial episteme, has played its role in the construction of race as a place of decision between human and non-human. While the field of environmental philosophy and the wider field of the environmental humanities has given some attention to questions of race, Laruelle's intervention may be useful for those who want to more centrally consider the intersection of race and ecology. It is clear from his own repeated references to racism in this work that future research is called for. While Laruelle's boldness in criticizing ecology as the new rival of philosophy may shock those who see ecology as the possible path to the salvation of the earth, it represents a relatively minority position of critical suspicion in the philosophical engagement with ecology. This is important precisely because, as we have sketched out here, there is no essential link between ecology and justice or ethics.

While Laruelle's focus on the level of abstraction means that he does not discuss possible ecological futures, activists and theorists have pointed out the past use of ecological ideas by fascists and the very probable use of ecology to justify the violence of ever harder borders, "resource management," and distinction of productive and unproductive peoples.[13] If ecological thinking is to offer a possible messianic vector for humanity, then it is important to undertake more critical interventions of these authoritarian and all-too philosophical elements of its thought and practice. The French *l'en-dernière-humanité,* translated throughout this book as "the in-the-last-humanity," takes a grammatical form similar to *l'en-soi* or "the in-itself," a concept common in modern and contemporary European philosophy. In *The Last Humanity* Laruelle creates the concept of "the in-the-last-humanity" as a way of conditioning ecology through an undoing of its role in the overrepresentation of the human. For the in-the-last-humanity signals the impossible relation of humanity to the authorities that try to regulate it, to manage it, to place it within a world where this person is more human than that person.

There is a pervasive sense that the world is ending. The ecology of climate change speaks to us of this crisis. And yet the very world that is ending is the world founded upon decision; founded upon the antiblack racism and misogyny of the overrepresentation of the human; the slaughter and suffering of non-human animals; and the reduction of the biosphere to economic use; and the continued reproduction of that world through this very same suffering and violence. The task facing the last humanity, the last of our humanity, is to call forth another end of the world. Not its reform, not its descent into greater barbarism, but an end of world as such in favor of a more open universe that includes a fragile and real earth. This is the great task that the confrontation between ecology and philosophy makes visible to us today and to which non-philosophy offers its tools.

FOREWORD

Here is what is at stake: to define man and other living things within the general framework of ecology—instead of through the traditional framework of philosophy—and thereby transform our concept of ecology. This displacement describes three ecological aspects using the minimum of philosophy: life without daily guidance, thinking without metaphysics, rigor without positive biology. The paradox of such an ecology—which can be said to be both "negative" in a weak sense, that of the "least," and as "fully-employed" in a strong sense, making use of these abstractions or those subtractions—is posited and resolved by a contemporary modeling, meaning a quantum modeling of the immanent history of the living. They are considered from the angle of their lived experience [vécu] through a very broad ecology as a new science, less biological than it is quantum, less empirical than it is transcendental, and which takes as its object the "lived-without-life" [vécu-sans-vie] as the abyssal ground (or "collapse") of the living, developing in the form of three continuously linked phases or even stages that want to make themselves autonomous and even return to philosophy. Such a mutation of ecological rationality, based on the algebra of complex or imaginary numbers, requires the creation of new terms or a regifting of meaning to old ones. This journey of life begins with the living in their being "lived-without-life," transforms them into aleatory subjects as products of their quantification, and then into generic clones through their relationship to the Universe. Clones are not biological here, they are the lived [les vécus] defined by three fundamental traits, they are generic rather than individual, random rather than strictly deterministic, and sexed [sexués], indexed, or measured according to the dimension of the Universe rather than to the dimension of the World. This new ecological science describes three phases or objects for the lived, the "In-sistence" that links them to the Earth, the "Ex-sistence" that links them to the World, and "Cloning" that links them to the Universe. So three sites [*lieux*] for the lived: the Earth which brings the collapse of the lived(-without-life) to the surface of the living, the World which marginalizes the lived as a horizon, and the Universe which, by verticalizing the lived, completes the addition of them to itself.

The first three chapters describe the degrowth of philosophy threatened with ruin by ecology. The fourth exposes the antinomy itself within the structure of philosophy's degrowth by ecology and in the principle of its quantum solution, then further on in chapter six, in the form of a science of the lived set out in their diverse phases. Chapter five sets out what the heart of the whole generic-quantum matrix is, the in-the-last-humanity or the lived-for-the-Universe, meaning the irreducible distinction of generic humanity and the rest of the living (but also irreducible to every theology), a humanity that under-determines all representations and gives them their vectoriell form.[1] We will have recognized the existence of a quantum of humanity that in no way excludes the ever-changing, undulating nature of the lived, this being the principle of a "Planck" ecology. Chapter six restates the entire quantification of the lived as well as cloning of a specifically philosophical kind.

Finally, the last chapter draws some ethical conclusions on the basis of an important difference, the defense of human life totally before-priority and the defense of animals and plants as priority. Finally, this ethics for life is based upon three principles that are said to be "of the least." This indicates not weakness but a good, theoretically rigorous dose of the two variables of exploitation and respect, the second always prevailing in-the-last-instance in the form of the in-the-last-humanity and orienting ethics in the direction of a reduction to the minimum of exploitation.[2] These principles constitute humanity's least risk or maximum safeguard, the least suffering for animals, the least use for plants, and the least exploitation of the Earth's resources. It is obvious that these three forms of the least add up to a collective effect for the living things it specifies (man, animals, etc.), as being the focus that decides each time on their addition and turns itself into the one that carries it all, but while taking account of the before-priority of humans in this collective task. This ethics of life is quantum rather than "negative," in the sense that it minimizes the possible harm threatening the living and maximumly defends them.

INTRODUCTION

For those who eat little, by choice or by necessity
For those who think little out of sufficiency
For those who are hungry for theory
A craving for concepts and theorems

A Thought Experiment on Ecology

We present a fundamental thesis regarding humans defined within the framework of a new ecology as clones-in-transit from the Earth to the Universe instead of subjects thrown-into-the-world, into Being, or into history. Then a second principal thesis regarding ecology as a science formalized quantumly and defined by its dependence on humans as their in-the-last-humanity. Finally, a third thesis that brings them together, clones are living subjects in general and among them they are humans in particular, as they are entangled in a new ecological science that spreads them out from the Earth they originate from so as to be thrown, indexed, and measured in the Universe. Due to a gnostic inspiration, with the effects that accompany it, we are required to weave these three theses in a more analytical way. The whole is an eco-fiction, a new ecological science parallel to science-fiction.

Ecology is gradually emerging as a universal thought rivaling philosophy. It also claims to struggle for a better life at the most concrete levels and to be able to regulate it. Ecology combines a concern for morals and wisdom regarding the body that is proper to the Ancients, it struggles against capitalism while also having become invasive like it. But as a way of thinking—and it is in this respect that it interests us—it has taken inhabitation upon the Earth as the last reference for existence without going beyond [*dépasser*] it toward the Universe. Ecology has instead moved back from Being-in-the-world toward the Earth as philosophy's superficial place and has not tried to go beyond the Copernican revolution as it could have tried to do if it had not remained fixed in a positivist manner to the Earth due to its lack of imagination and its fear of fiction. Hence its stifling prosaicness, its quibbling mediocrity, its political chattering. Its contribution to philosophy's decline—so that this greater thought could follow—has not always been seen. How can we get out of this confusing situation, make the new affect in it grow, affects as much as resources, and restore the assistance of philosophy it deserves and that it has deserted? But what philosophy does the Earth deserve (if it has had one, up until now) that has not been borrowed from and destined for heaven, where it has stored its treasures? Let us take up the problem from the beginning in the form of a first axiom. The beginning is also the middle and the end for a living thing that touches on philosophy as well as ecology, on science as well as art, on religion as well as politics. This living thing that is more cumbersome than the others—both in terms of its banality and its way of wanting to interfere in everything— is probably man. Let us assume that man is the only one of the living who cannot reconcile himself to being the first or the last between them, but either the *before-the-first* by way of excess over priority, or the *after-the-last* by way of weakness or collapse. These are two ways of making a certain exception to the common order of things. This state claimed by the living human, generically sexed, by which it under-determines the rest of creation, is what is called the clone, not in any biological sense, but in its humanity of-the-last-instance or as we will say "in-the-last-humanity." Man is a clone "in-the-last-humanity," this is a definition of the latter. It is true that the after-the-first and the before-the-last are not very seductive and arouse only a few thoughts. The last judgments belong to the clone by right because the clone is for the first and last time a prior-priority before the priority of animals, plants, and minerals, or it is after-the-last humanity or after-ultimacy for the first and last time and so after animals and plants (perhaps its immortality). But let us leave here these chiasma and entanglements which were only intended to quantumly trouble the common representation of ecology.

The curve of its growing demands leads ecology into a theoretical contradiction with philosophy, a different antinomy than those antinomies Kant dealt with, grounded, and argued with on a scientific basis but that were also old, positivist, and poorly adapted to our problems and too dialectical in style. If Kant refined his antinomies, perhaps too much, we can still refine ours differently, in a less classically rationalist way, so that it welcomes finer distinctions and mixtures, entanglements, and noncommutativities, and draw out its essence from its symptoms, an essence that we can read otherwise than as an injunction to put it back into the straightjacket of ontology. Following the example of substituting ethics (Levinas) or biology (Bergson) in place of the old philosophical ontology, life and its ecological context are thematized here as a new object deciding for a non-philosophy or requiring a nonstandard thought. This means creating the notion of an ecological era of thought, a new ecological science based upon quantum modeling that is introduced between ecology and philosophy. It is a change of terrain: we move from the ontological duality of Being/beings to ecology based upon the new duality accessible only to quantum physics and capable of dissolving the antinomy, that of the Universe and the lived as a collapse that short-circuits the duality of Being and beings and places the world in brackets.

This great suspension of the world and life, their being put out of play without Husserl's attempted phenomenological return, forces us to model in a theoretical and quasi-experimental way what quantum physicists (Einstein, Schrödinger) call a "thought experiment" made for this occasion with regard to the concept of the living—from man to the universe and including the famous cat—and that leads to the ecological and quantum redefinition of the living as clones that are non-biological but conceptual. We seem to be reversing the metaphysical notion of "human nature" into that of a "physically modeled humanity."

So there are new notions to be introduced: that of the minimal quantum of humanity we set at the base of every ecology, that of the lived-without-life that we fashion (rather than living things so reduced), and finally that of clones which we place at the end of ecological transformations. The clone is the entity that ends that journey which goes from the living by way of the lived-without-life to the generic clone, no longer having anything biological about it. Let us remember that we are partially conducting a quantum thought experiment on philosophy and especially on ecology, so not a philosophical thought experiment, directly from the understanding, and therefore transcendental in its ultimate dimension. It begins with a reduction of the data that living things are in their superposed lived experience, and then continues with two ordeals bound together that the lived-without-life will have undergone in order to pass to the state of the quantum and generic clone. A double ordeal: 1. having passed through all the steps of the quantum process in the form of a vectoriell and complex matrix or equipped with the imaginary number (a vectoriell preparation of the superposed states of a system, its being sent into a channel that localizes and distributes it, its collisions and its disjunctions that are its second life but invisible to this one, finally its exit as a probable subject); 2. having been indexed to the dimension of the Universe that gives the aleatory subject its completed status as a clone, which can now be called generic and not at all biological, even less so quantum. Clones will only be complete or achieved when their lived experience has passed the stage of its gestation as an aleatory subject and when it has faced its birth in the Universe or its generic state. So ends what the gnostics thought should "arise" from [naitre de] the Earth into the Universe, what they could have called the "great tunnel" in memory of the quantum tunnel.

It is not surprising that we define clones as forms of the lived that are quantumly transformed from the living, particles as it were of the lived-without-life but sexed and that inhabit the Universe's dimension.

Rather than stranger-philosophers making their way in the World from crossroads to crossroads, they are the wandering inhabitants of the Universe and move in a way that is both jerky and fluid.[1] Manipulators of algebras, hypotheses, and fictions, they are in themselves the new science of ecology and its ethics exploring the empire of clones. Eco-fiction runs alongside science-fiction on its most intimate edge and solves the antinomy of ecology and philosophy. At a different magnitude than the Cogito's, the maxim of these objects of science that have become objects of knowledge, abandoning the already ancient words, "the starry sky above me, the moral law within me," for the newer, "we humans thrown into the empty environment of the universe, guardians of all other living things, we contemplate the starry sky of ecology lived within us and outside of us."

From Aleatory Subjects to Sexed Clones or Ordinary Messiahs

The central problem of ecology, when it is not treated in a ratiocinate and empirical way at the limit of media-friendly vulgarity, remains that of the living human being and its place (if not its work) in the Universe rather than in the World. A complicated set of fusions and distinctions, of non-separabilities and separabilities, of intertwined relationships between man on the one hand, and on the other hand the animal, plants, and the earth. Everything that constitutes an analytic of life taken from the new antinomy of ecology and philosophy is presented here according to the quantum operator of the imaginary number. This account deploys the two principal theses or the two pillars of this essay, one strictly quantum or matrix-esque, the reduction of all living things as aleatory subjects to vectors and to the imaginary number, the specifically generic other and cloning of non-biological lived experiences, up to the ultimate sexual cloning of the lived human.

In this transcendental theory, the materials of the quantum and philosophy conjugate themselves as two halves of a theoretical device that associates the abscissa of the quantum apparatus and the ordinate of the transcendental apparatus that work together to produce subject-clones from the material of the living, as if Cartesian coordinates had been raised to a higher use as a double dimension of a quantum ecology. The antinomy of ecology and philosophy can only be resolved in the process of generation and its phases, the parturition of childbirth, the genericness of birth. Finally, we could add the summation of individual life, death, and the return to the invisible . . .

1. The first fundamental thesis is in the style of quantum physics, but *infra-structural*, and has already been outlined in other terms by Marx. This thesis says that *man is an animal that makes animality human* or by extension and variation, *man is a plant that humanizes plantness, man is an earthly being that humanizes the earth*. This thesis is made up of two autonomous statements based on two variables occupying inverted places in order to form these two statements. All at once it is a renunciation of "human nature" and even its philosophical representation, because man now appears as a variable to be conjugated with the other variable, at least that of the animal, in two statements that are themselves inverted. And he appears as an aleatory subject, undetermined in his face as a human being. Since there is no longer any human nature in the classical sense, there are only local effects of nature or of a philosophical essence that must be taken into account without exaggerating them in what is now only an aleatory calculation of lived experience. This first stage is a kind of still anonymous or indeterminate parturition, a birth that has begun and is not yet complete.

Can we turn this first statement of the thesis upside down or reverse it as we did before? *The animal is a human (or humanized) being that makes the human being an animal or animalized him, etc.?* Undoubtedly, but only on the condition that the products of these variables are lowered to the state of becomings, conjugating the two terms of the statement. To humanize the animal, these two statements are possible in a combinatory and plausible way from the point of view of phenomenal life. These variables are no longer quantitative or fixed essences, they are affected by the imaginary number and are already non-commutative becomings. It is a matter of further analyzing these statements and their products in man and animal, including them in a device that sketches a new ecological era of thought taking its leading role in place of philosophy. It is philosophy's theoretical displacement by ecology that wants to assume from now on its guiding function. But this displacement is only the first phase of a massive earthquake.

There is still something more required by combinatory quantum physics that will look for even finer variables than man and animal: that of the sexual difference acting in these two variables. Let us try it on at least one of them, the human rather than the animal, at the risk of scandalous statements that will temporarily complete the table of quantum sexual calculation. *Man (in the sense of the masculine) masculinizes woman (making the feminine masculine) who inversely feminizes man.* Beautiful statement! We suspected that, even biologically, it is not revolutionary and in marriage or the homogenized couple it ends up in a pleonasm. This thesis is no longer contradictory if it focuses on becomings rather than on relationships of essence. If the reversibility of the products of the variables erases the sexual difference that some would have liked to be irreversible, non-commutative, unchangeable, the quantum point of view makes it return but in the form of a universal noncommutativity of subjects and then clones.

Our point of view is neither that of hormonal and genetic mixtures or relationships, it is that of a rigorous transcendental kind of knowledge that focuses on *a priori* knowledge of the objects of experience, or that takes all the previous distinctions as *a priori* pairs that mediatize the relationship of objective knowledge to experience. Rather than laughing at it, it is necessary to appreciate the combinatorial rigor without exception of this quantum sexual calculation, the conjugated force of the two properties assumed by a subject = X. This subject is the non-separable fusion of man/woman equal in this function as variables, their reciprocal noncommutativity and their added universal noncommutativity makes them unable to be exchanged with their subject = X as their fusion, or which detaches them in some way from their subject and prepares them to be sent and treated in those channels which represent their location in the form of superposed states. The sexual quantum is based on the entanglement that binds all these various couples over the greatest distance, we will see that it is the Universe's indexation which makes this calculation incalculable.

2. The second, equally fundamental thesis, is called generic and superstructural or the *generic cloning* of the aleatory subject that has just been produced in the preceding. It says that *the aleatory subject produced by the quantum process of the infra-structure, whether man or animal, masculine or feminine, is now indexed to the universal form of objectivity that is no longer the World but the Universe as a dimension of superposition, and so forms a generic clone that exceeds* [dépassse] *the World through this indexing*. The clone is not only an aleatory subject produced under the distant condition of superposition from which it is first deduced. It is also now the object of a new operation that is very different from the first and which nevertheless implies superposition for a second time, but as a messianic axis or verticality of objectivity or of the Universe. This aleatory subject returns, in a way, "in" or "under" itself, but this time indexed to the dimension of objectivity or of the Universe. Paradoxically, this operation is not a transcendence that is philosophically doubled or raised-over [*sur-élève*]. Rather, it is an ascendency that is necessarily doubled or lowered-over [*sur-baissée*] instead of raised-over. It is a second birth, not only taking place within a matrix but as generic or messianic. The generic clone surpasses [*dépasse*] the World without trans-gressing it, in a transfinite way, through the ascendency of a circle circulating infinitely in itself from its own shattered collapse or "quarter turn" (Lacan), oscillating between collapse and ascendency, like the wave

that carries and guides itself as the particle that it is for-itself. What a mistake of perspective for the all-too-humans who always want to make themselves bigger, to believe that the stars are "above me" when they are always halfway up, already too low, already falling or fallen and lowered, because they have emerged from a collapse "under" me, a starry sky fallen "below" me, if we can put it this way. Didn't Kant himself make a mistake, even though he was connecting the mine and the sky in a single, doubled gaze? "The upright man is the glory of God," says a Father of the Church.[2]

What can I say, except that this man standing there is already a broken man, smaller than he thinks he is? Try to form for yourself the statement: "The upright woman is the glory of God." There is something absurd about this formula or it expresses a macho irony, and yet we want to restore woman's messianic dignity. Humans who "believe" in Heaven are victims of the Earth, their fervor or their leap actually fails "before" Heaven. The now eco-generic lived is only closed onto itself through a non-philosophical circle, lowered or crushed "in itself" by a collapse. The collapse is not "sexual difference" or the complement that separates and connects living things to each other as a recorded datum and (pre)programmed in terms of biological origins. It is the factor that "makes" an origin, the "origenetic" point at which the biological is raised-over and is opened to the future universe. It affects through a radical "degrowth" or under-determines the production of the generic lived, degrowing before its specification according to kind. To under-determine is apparently to provoke, more deeply to take its origin (as its flight) within a collapse. The collapse is the trace of the universal presence of the imaginary number in every intention and in every causality of representation. This is undoubtedly the authentic meaning of the microscopic, or the quantum, the particle being only a collapse of the object through which it opens itself to its objectivity or its "decoherence." We must think quantumly, in incoherence, through wave collapse, before thinking coherence, the place of all illusions. To grasp or more precisely to be grasped by a quivering that is itself without origin, the very-first oscillation of an ocean, cradle, or womb that occupies all the space of the body, ebb, and flow that come to beat its shores. This seismic tremor of the collapse that shakes the living in its lived wombs is not that last one which would complete the tearing away of the placenta, nor even the first one, but the before-first, which any living being would feel as a "shudder" announcing a coming parturition in its "pregnant" state by the virtue of its quantum gravity alone making it into a lowered-over being.

As stated by the first thesis, and especially more for humans than animals (even if the problem extends to couples of all species), men and women legally split the human into two variables that dismember their mixture and makes possible their conjugal fusion as a result of their ability to be conjugated and not because of their institutional and legal conjugation, further fine-tuning the difference between living things as now a sexual duality in a quantum and ecological environment. The duality of human and feminine clones begins a new conjugation whose material is now the aleatory subjects indexed to the Universe as clones but who are split into two clones, no longer as aleatory subjects but as generic clones. 1. The masculine and the feminine are two aleatory lived subjects produced by the quantum and matrix process, this is their specificity as quantum probability, 2. this difference in quantum probability comes under a generic difference of indexing and cloning, 3. this generic trait of cloning is in turn modulated by sexual difference properly so-called, which is now the sexual difference of clones and not that of living things considered as earthly or "worldly" lived realities that have to be made intelligible. If the process of placing within a matrix produces an aleatory subject, the second phase is that of the generic clone, specified a first time as either a human or as an animal, a third time as completing the cloning by way of the sexual duality which, if it is to be made intelligible, is never a simple sexual difference. Sexual cloning reaches the "incalculable generic sex" rather than the "philosophical sex" where much of the thought of this subject resides. Its objective or subjectively, aleatory, matrix-esque basis concerns the lived human or even that of the animal rather than the living "man" or "animal", but it needs to be quantumly completed through an indexing to the scale of the Universe where both men and women participate when it comes to their lived realities, instead of with regard to their lives of mixtures and exchanges. Let us repeat again that this is a science that seeks to explain the human ecological kingdom of life through a thought experiment that connects man to the Universe, which is the great *transcendental vinculum* but lowered-over, and that considers the couple and conjugality as a "scientific sacrament." This is the invisible path from the living to its clone, passing through the substitution of the lived-without-life for the living, that of the generic in a quantum matrix, that of the sexual cloning of the lived in all the avatars of representation.

If we now allow that spectrum of possibilities to unfold from three living things (or four with the Earth) that conjugate two by two, we can imagine the explosion of this sort of combinatorial in aleatory terms that form the system of generic clones which, all of them, men, animals, or plants (including here the earth as a "metaphorical" mineral life) are capable of completing the work begun by the *infra*-structural matrix of the under-determination of philosophical representations. These data are initially treated as quantumly prepared materials and then under-determined as generic clones, not to mention the clones of a philosophical origin, about which we will say a word later. The correlate of the infrastructure is an aleatory subject, man or animal, which once indexed to the dimension of the universe, becomes a generic clone. The clones fill the Universe and constitute the in-the-last-humanity as the set of messiahs, they are almost reflected on themselves (or "in" themselves by the dimension of the universe) through the collapsed superposition that unfailingly binds the Universe to this collapse. The Universe is the cogito of the clones, concerning which everyone must be able to say, "I think the Universe, therefore I am a clone." There is no metaphysical human nature, but a multiplicity of cloned states, of lived-without-life cloning that inhabits the Universe as the new Earth of the living.

The Three Dimensions of Transcendental Ecology: Earth, World, Universe

We, living humans, are identifiable by three systems of phenomenological coordinates, and not according to theological ones. The gnostics have described these according to three possible places, three disproportionate ways of being embedded [*englobants*]: the Earth which is habitable by all living things in their most exact definition of "down-to-earth" [*terre-à-terre*], the Universe uninhabitable by the living but desirable in their current definition as clones or messiahs, and between these two, the inhabited but hateful World that is dominated by the living-beings-in-transit called humans. Embeddedness? This is not certain; it is also a matter of enclosures of quantum coherence or decoherence if we abandon the philosophical system of reference. Living beings of all species, we have our three fundamental ecological objects: the Earth which is the I [*moi*] of the living, the World which is their body, and the Universe which is their sky. These three orders structure transcendental ecology, like Kant's transcendental dialectic, as the I, the World, and God. But with very different structures and functions, ecology, gnosis, and science-fiction have renewed our understanding of life and humanity in particular. The most profound triplicity that affects us is that of these three disproportionate ways of being embedded: the Earth and the Universe that de-coordinates us or de-situates us, one through the collapse that works it, the other through the infinite where it is lost, the World finally that occupies the point of their crossing and which, to the contrary, condemns us to inscribe ourselves within restrictive coordinates.

As the original reference point for life, the Earth is not only immobile as it is for those philosophers who always begin too high in Heaven as Platonist astronomers, guardians for a herd of celestial mares, but the Earth in-sists rather than exists under our feet and even already below us, shaken, crushing onto itself through an algebraic earthquake (square root of −1), a collapse whose aftershocks will shake the highest levels of Heaven itself, meaning it will bring it down to its center of gravity. The Earth is the unity of a ground and a collapse that collapses onto itself and contracts itself, it makes of us living beings bent over the aridity of the land [*glèbe*], brought low and shaken by the bad winds of time that it blows into the World thus bent over the Earth as a chasm that breaths it in, thrown to a horizontal fate by a fleeting horizon toward which we endlessly tend in an immanent way without being able to assimilate it. The contracted fault that opens the Earth in principle is defined as translocalized, the essence of a collapse. It also affects the World in a way that is no longer underground, but rises and extends itself as a surface. Horizontal in-static [*in-statico*], it inclines beyond the horizon and motions toward the Universe. The Earth split into a semi-open space that will have fascinated those philosophies determined to live within the World. But however short it may be, the transcendence of the World is as if it were withdrawn from the great messianic vertical transcendence of the Universe that it is measured by. The collapse divines the Earth before reflecting itself in itself as a World and out of itself as a great messianic vertical of the Universe that the World is indexed by with all its living things. The earthquake of the collapse places the first transcendence of the World in the abyss as short or finite. This fault extends in a trans-horizontal way, the World coming on top of the Earth's fracture and originating from this abyss, as if it were withdrawing the Earth from the greatest transcendence, that of the Universe yet nevertheless lowered. The living things that came to life in the earthquake of birth and were exiled as clones come back to life in the immortal form of death, they form a circle that seals the living as clones "in-life-and-in-death." It is important to be buried in the Earth, each dead person makes his vault there, the other his tomb, another leaves his ashes or his rhizome, like a hierarchy of the dead, each one a collapse that returns to inhabit a clone that buries itself there as if life returned to itself in the lop-sided circle of death.

As for the World, it is the unity of a facial depth and a horizontality, this time bending the living over a horizon that pours into an opening where it vanishes and renews itself, in a state of flight or disappearance.

The Universe is yet another curvature to which we are indexed within and outside of ourselves and by which we are measured. It is not copied from the first, no longer does it inscribe the finitude of ecological life that takes place on Earth as philosophy does from its World context in order to measure it to itself, it is true but with too little difference. The Universe, also curved by the weight of the Earth but open or infinite, is the right measure for any possible ecology that would present itself, thus corrected, as a future or eco-fiction.

The disproportion of these ways of being embedded in no way prevents the collapse that secretly acts at the ground of the Earth to pass on its replicas from one to the other and consequently does not prevent it from lowering the entire architecture of the building in relation to its philosophical and phantasmic theological height. We must learn to distinguish the Being-in-the-world that occupied past philosophers a great deal from the duality of extremes that surround the World, that of the living-for-the-Earth and the lived-for-the-Universe, an adequate duality with the distinction derived from it of the living and the lived-without-life. Of these two very different affects, Being-in-the-world represents, as usual, the philosophical confusion of a fractured ground and a narrow opening. Being-in-the-world is precisely the fusion or ambiguity of a duality that will have been continuously understand in a philosophical spirit and not a scientific one. The Universe is the anti-Earth and the Earth is the anti-Universe, but they are able to be conjugated together and give rise to non-commutative products rather than to the World. Gnosis here anticipates the good duality of the variables. Ecological finitude is that of the earth—may we be spared the accusation of an agrarian regression that Heidegger was rightly the subject of, even if it is from the spirit of the Earth that certain regressive aspects of an ecology that is not ours are born—while the earth takes its share of infinitude from the lowered infinity of the Universe that the ecological dimension is indexed to. However, let us recognize that the distinction is difficult between an ecology in the spirit of quantum rationality and a ratiocinate ecology in a Newtonian spirit, as we will see, and not without some risk of confusion. The collapse of the collapse acts through three effects that are all lowering or devastating falls for transcendence: a sinkhole or collapse effect that sucks humans in, an opening effect or surface horizon around which the small opening of the emerging World only emerges to fold and fall back into an open space of invisibility, finally, it is in this earthly collapse, but mediated or relaunched by this semi-opening as toward the World, that the great vertical opening of the Universe will be implanted, which the collapse affects as its foundation or as the source of its depth, forcing this verticality to be lowered as well.

To extend the sphere of ecology from the Earth to the Universe by passing beyond the World, to introduce the Universe into ecology as the parameter that extends it into the depths of infinity and obliges us to understand the facticity of life as a collision, is a way of making ecology fictional, not speculative. On the contrary it is a de-specularizing of ecology or one ridding it of its mirror, of discharging it from its identification work, of conquering a "lowered" universality that philosophy would no longer be the paradigm and master of. Ecology can only grow in people's minds as a new messianic paradigm under two conditions. Undoubtedly through the picture of the excesses of the destruction human life's natural place, which forms the basis of an ecology of protest, incrimination, and demand, whatever its political, economic, or aesthetic form. More profoundly, but in a less apparent way, through the progressive discovery of a new dual dimension of the collapsed Earth and the lower-over Universe, of the living and the lived as well, which "sounds" gnostic if we want to avoid the Copernican considerations of a prematurely philosophical or worldly essence. The way Plato distinguishes between the types of humanity or philosophers, we will distinguish between the friends of the Earth and the friends of the Universe. Kant has his way of detecting this duality of ecological variables while relying on a still planetary localization that the World remains the hinge of, "within the world and outside of the it" as he puts it in a unitary way as rationalism itself. However, he puts his finger on a meta-Copernican duality since the experience of this very concrete paradigm of a new opposition; the formula written by the Silesian miners at the bottom and from the bottom of their tunnel, the duality of the "salt mine" and the "starry sky above me." This duality displaces the one that Newtonian physics had established. Kant can read the duality of the variables, on the one hand the sky covered over, and therefore experimental, as the natural laws of Copernicanism, and on the other hand the open sky or heart, the moral law, and possibly read them through an inversion near their conditions for access. For their part, the gnostics practice a similar kind of more modestly meta-lunar cut, despite their psychologism they knew how to take the Other Man or Stranger to a completely different dimension at the same time as they let the World created by an evil God sink into its ruins. As for us, finally, the non-philosophical heirs of gnosis, we have the experience of a new crossed duality or of a chiasmus, that of the quantum window, so as in a blink of an eye to jump into the lowered infinity of the universe, no more, a quantum microflash in response to the Greek macro-flash that illuminates the philosophical cosmos.

Generic human clones, women and men, replenish the universe, constitute the in-the-last-humanity, they are almost reflected on themselves (or "in" themselves) through the Universe's dimension between the collapse where they fall and from which they rise, and the Universe they are haunted by. The Universe is the cogito of clones, about which everyone must be able to say, "we think the Universe, we are the haunting of the Universe from the fault of the Earth, its clones, its messiahs, and its wanderers." There is no human nature delivered by metaphysics, but a multiplicity of cloned states, of the lived-without-life, of messiahs who touch the Earth of the living and stop there only to die and be eternally buried there.

1
IN SEARCH OF A MESSIANIC ECOLOGY

Between Biology and Philosophy

We are looking for a very narrow path between biology and philosophy that is not controlled by spontaneous philosophy or positive molecular biology, but which nevertheless uses both at once modeled in a new "ecological" conjugation that turns to quantum theory. The philosophy of life is more about its immanence (Hegel, Nietzsche, Bergson, Deleuze, Henry), but suffers from its usual "sufficiency." The science of life, molecular biology, has given rise to a first quantum formalization (Bohr, Schrödinger). A new ontic theory of life obviously cannot be our object, but the knowledge of life as it interests humanity is our one and only "onto-logical" object. Our project has a "transcendental" aspect and focuses on the knowledge of life itself. We are not involved with either of the two kinds of solutions, each antithetical and positive in their way. And yet we will require both (almost) simultaneously as productive forces of knowledge, a certain nonpositive quantum modeling of life and a certain philosophy of life that is no longer dominant and sufficient.

Why this complicated strategy, what is at stake? It is twofold: to reformulate an ecological problematic as the context for the knowledge of life, and human life in particular. On the first point, can ecology become a competing project with philosophy? What are the conditions for a rigorous thought of life that gives it its full ecological amplitude? On the second point, it is indirectly a question regarding the knowledge of universal life within human life, but also regarding human life and human knowledge within all animal and plant life. How is it possible to break deterministic causality at the risk of returning to the Great Everything of a universal ecology? It is precisely a question of suspending this other antithetical between determinism and a vicious causality and establishing a new anthropic principle (of non-sufficiency) in the ruins of ecological anthropology. However, on the condition that there is a decisive nuance: the anthropic principle is to be in-the-last-instance and ecology is to be a thought "in-the-last-humanity."

Of all the aporias that clutter thought, few have become as insistent as the difference between man and animal more generally, and then adding the plant as well it becomes a circular and vicious conception of the MAP system (Man, Animal, Plant). This abstract generality, specific to everyday conversation as well as to the philosophers, requires a radical clearing of thought, but by no means a *tabula rasa*. It is not a question of erasing all difference through a summary rejection of metaphysics, but just that of finding a non-sufficient principle for the distribution of the living within life and outside of it. The indefinite, asymptotic approach of man and animal seem to us to be as unthinking in their absolute difference and to be part of the same conversational philosophy. We oppose "Being-in-the-last-humanity" of all life to the circular nature of a hermeneutic ecology as much as to its casual linearity, and we say that "in-the-last-humanity" can be said also as the "man's before-priority" over the animal and the plant. From causality's point of view, this is a paradox since the two meanings seem opposed to one another, but each of them takes on some nuance that makes them compatible. In any case, what is excluded is man's metaphysical priority over the two other kinds of life, his assumed superiority and his sufficiency of measure for the others. There is a plane of immanence of life where each of the three kinds is equal to the two others and this plane is defined by the univocity of the *lived-without-life that is imposed by the quantum postulate of its discretion as the minimum threshold below which it is impossible for life to descend.* This threshold has only been approached by molecular biology (in the form of a code of life) for a positive science of life. But we posit the quantum of the lived as the threshold that makes life accessible to a science that is generic this time. Of course, this discreetness of the minimum of the lived conforming to the quantum spirit is contrary to speculation and makes a "speculative ecology" impossible in the excessive sense, even if it aims at a formalization in-the-last-humanity of life rather than a Hegel-style speculation upon its Great Circle.

Traditional ecology's foundations are differential and naturalistic, enclosed within eco-logical difference, they go back at least to Aristotle and continue to legitimize its political fury that plays out across the media. The irritating criticism of ecological "movements" and the little bit of thought that is hidden there in its well-known "empathy" is hardly sufficient. It would still be necessary to update the possibility of ecology inscribing itself within the immanence of life in these three paradigmatic forms: human, animal, and plant. As well as being necessary to elucidate the deadly and protective role that humans play in this ecological triangle. The mass of unclear assumptions is justified by a theoretical bric-a-brac, by almost philosophical considerations, and by the usual kinds of ignorance that philosophy devoted to the World's inertia, maintained in all good conscience. However embedded the eco-logical difference may be, however varied its modalities and dimensions, it is itself destined to be auto-erasing as a structure. It shows little real amplitude and effective work, preferring to speculate on technology, Being, the climate, and the exploitation of nature. Reduced to the denunciation of the devastating relationships between humans and animals in the arena of plants and the Earth's climate, to the problems of humanity's survival, it fuels media, political, and ideological unrest, which the greatest speculations can hardly struggle against, those concerning man and his Being-in-the-world, on the body and mind, on matter and memory. A dissociation affects it, subjected to the extremes by Darwinian scientific naturalism, which leads to animal culture and pathos, and elsewhere by a religious and creationist nostalgia, able to be identified in a too quick and ready-made understanding of man's indivisible essence.

Note for the Reader

As has already been said, this essay is not based on the various references or information found in the disciplinary or epistemological field of ecology. Instead it is a "prolegomena for any ecology that can present itself as a future." Thus, the construction of a problematic or a "building" intended to shelter isolated or crossed theoretical species, some of which may be in the process of disappearing, becoming more scarce, and degrowth, like philosophy and metaphysics, while others are in the process of an ascending growth, like ecology itself and the sciences that support it. The often combinatorial style of this project explains why the main concepts are symbolized by initials or acronyms for ease of reading and that should be read as simply opening or deploying them discursively as a symbol for the concepts. For example, M, A, P reads as "man, animal, plant," but M/A reads as "the duality of man and animal," and MA as "the fusion of man-animal or of man as also an animal."

Ecology versus Philosophy: The New Antinomy

"Ecology" is the symptom of a double process that involves multiple sites and disciplines, the Earth and its inhabitants. A contradictory process, and perhaps self-contradictory as well, in which the plaintiffs each seek to establish a court that will vindicate them. So another dispute of a higher level is engaged, beyond strictly ecological debates, between a declining philosophy and a rising and rival ecology. This double level each time implies a trial and a counter-trial that are distributed like a patchwork. Whether we take it from one or the other of its parts, we see a constant variation in the local relationships of force, sometimes to the benefit of the newest and weakest, sometimes to the benefit of a more global force [*pression*] known as "capitalism." If we look now for the means mobilized by all parties then the dispute changes in terms of theoretical scope and style, it mobilizes Marxism, Nietzcheanism, and Foucauldianism. We have not one, but several toolboxes. However, one is missing, which is that of a universal science, a context that is specifically physical and contemporary, such that without this intervention ecology would inexorably continue the fall (if we can put it this way) that it began with and can present a rather vulgar face. Although at these counter-trials all living things are summoned as witnesses for the prosecution, it is—as we understand it in a narrow and media-friendly sense and in a way that is still very philosophical—an ecology of spontaneous protest and a demand that could well become, who knows, a personal hypothesis, the equivalent of what the Reformation was for the old Catholic and Aristotelian world but now in the field of the perception of life by the living. It would still have to be grounded as a possible new life. But let's leave it there.

Let it be understood that what we call an "antinomy" is a conflict not without exchanges, a dispute not without confusion between two contemporary postures of thought, one of which is in the making, so therefore in a less narrow and rationalist sense, and one more complex than the Kantian antinomy that was dialectically prepared to receive a rationalist solution. One might object that we too are preparing the antinomy so that it necessarily receives a quantum solution that is worthy of contemporary thought, of its rationality and not of rationalism. What we are aiming for as an antinomy is not resolved in a rationalist way but tolerates postmodern ambiguities. It is inevitable, each era has its answers and the questions that are adapted to them but the terms and their relationships will almost all change as will the content and solution of the antinomy. We must be persuaded that it is better to anticipate the coming of an antinomy that is still barely perceptible between philosophy and ecology, decided and well designed by those who see it coming, than to deny it on the basis of phenomena that are already too old or irrelevant when they manifest themselves. We are forcing the appearance of an antinomy that seemed improbable on first sight. But this way of doing things corresponds to our way of doing things, it is not only the solution that is a utopia, it is the problem itself that seems to not yet exist. This is the art of "whistleblowers," those modern Cassandras, those from whom what we call philo-fiction and here eco-fiction would do well to draw inspiration, a function of watchmen and messiahs for philosophers who have lacked so much vigilance, even the best symptomatologists of them read the future in the womb of their cadaverized past.

To this end, we introduce the notion *of a Pure Quantum Reason as a solution to the antinomy, the concept of which must be seriously expanded and subtracted from the too narrow dimensions it is usually confined to.* All that will remain of Kant is enough to legitimate a certain similarity with him, not a copy of the Kantian dialectic or even a copy of quantum physics, "orthodox" or not. Quantum theory is our toolbox according to the established formula, theoretical tools that have changed considerably. But it always a matter of enclosure, from the box for Schrödinger's cat to De Broglie's photon box to Plato's theatrical cave, from the bubble chamber to the collider and from the particle tunnel to the Universe as a supercollider. An enclosure must always be pierced, the housekeepers of the Universe that physicists are know this and pass it on through something other than the wormholes that still remain in it. Is there nothing more noble and more human than these wormholes? Something like a messianic breakthrough into the Universe itself? That will have to be seen.

Let us assume that in modernity, the original trial, the party who decides with his complaint that a trial is to be held and that it is urgent to set up a tribunal, that of philosophers against the inhospitable environment of nature, which calls for its mastery and its possession, its "questioning" (Kant), but which in return also creates guilt for those humans who exploit it at will. Hence a later counter-trial that the Earth calls for against the most ruthless of its inhabitants who are thereby set in self-contradiction. It is the silent protest of animals, plants, the violent protest of the Earth itself against the lack of concern, the casualness and exploitation of its resources.

Philosophy nourishes a large part of ecology, which can only rise up as a new vision of life and thought, and not only, too easily, against

Cartesianism. There is in any case a duplicity of philosophy that in a homologous way internalizes ecology into its own internal conflict with itself. This means that, as a new form of the "misunderstanding of reason with itself" (Kant), it places us on the path of a problem that becomes sensible, that of an antithetics of reason that replaces older ones, also those of physicists, and whose true dimensions, ignored by their fighters who are manipulated by it, are those of a conflict within philosophy that proposes its traditional solutions, and of an emerging ecology that seeks to make a place for itself, that enters fully into this fight and intends to inaugurate a new kingdom finally proper to Human reason inasmuch as it must guide life in an immanent way rather than govern it.

We need a new post-rationalist "critique" to share the blame between the Earth and its inhabitants, perhaps to establish a universal peace treaty between philosophy and ecology. It is this conflict of Ecological Reason, regarding which we are trying to be "critical," that is, as it must be repeated after the other ones, a positive evaluation, with contemporary means and materials different from Kant's. The pure reason that is affected by this antinomy will be defined under quantum conditions that are capable of modeling this conflict and providing it with the means for a balanced solution. It is a "Pure" Quantum Reason but not at all a "speculative" one and not simply a "critical" one. Its quantum means, instead of Newtonian ones, eliminate speculation from the philosophy it mobilizes but equally eliminates the Kantian critique through the probability that it establishes in knowledge.

We thus propose to define upon new foundations, scientifically renewed and philosophically reformed, what Kant calls a peace treaty and the Ancients generally called an immanent "Life," both contemplative (*vita contemplativa*) and practical (*vita practica*). We call this peace a *vita ecologica*. It is therefore not a question of rethinking existing ecological disciplines and their traditional positive and metaphysical foundations through the introduction of new anthropological materials, recent and alarmist information on the "state of the planet," but of coming to a situation of "good neighborliness" for humans in the World and within the horizon of the Earth in the company of animals and plants under the double guard of the highest authorities of thought: the One, Being, the Other, and more recent forms of rationality from physics. However, we expect nothing like the evangelical sleep of the lion and the lamb side by side, the situation of humans and other living beings is not only too complex and mixed in appearance to find this satisfying but, as quantum physicists say, the situation is too "entangled" to be satisfied with this and other silly pap proper to a sleepwalking ecology. One of the difficulties in resolving this antimony lies in the state of entanglement of the ecological real, since we will assume that such a real of the microscopical order exists and disturbs macrobiological conceptuality without rendering it obsolete, because the quantum is sometimes applicable to macroscopic entities. This is the case with those still philosophical concepts of life and the living. We obviously do not do molecular biology (we will encounter this problem with the definition of a quantum of the lived and humanity), we quantize thinking concerning life; it is ecological discourse, not this living thing or that species, that supports this quantification or "placing in a superposition," this is why our own discourse will have a transcendental style and do so within the very same quantum. Such purely transcendental principles (not mixed with experience but which speak about it and for it, meaning the knowledge contained in the antinomy that we treat as a material) as those of superposition and noncommutativity, are necessary to make accessible in theory and in epistemology the physical-and-philosophical real of ecology that traditional philosophy or ecology left to itself hardly helps us to understand.[1]

Some will be offended that so much ambition is accompanied by our customary absence of references to the countless works that present themselves as "ecological," to our lack of information within the positive disciplines that serve as their ordinary justification. This is our style of intervention, it asks us not to confuse architecture with a philosophy of furniture, and the architect of those already future ruins of the ecological palace, which the Earth is, with an interior designer who arranges his pedestal tables with the best of taste. However, it is not a speculative ecology, we claim the right to a temptation that we hope to become an attempt of (as Nietzsche says) or even an eco-fiction. If it is speculative, and there will indeed be reason to make such a complaint, it is only in a banal sense and one distorted by its theoretical difficulty, for the rest is rather what we call a "thought experiment" on "pure" or "in-person" Ecological Reason through its aims and means, certainly not very empirical, which are taken from a quantum model rather than a Newtonian one as the "old critique" was. There has always been a little ecology and a little messianity together in history, we try to link them again in order to increase their amplitude properly within the immanence of a life. Ecology is here futural, it is not *of* this time even if we would want it to be *for* this time, it is an eco-fiction built from very distant philosophical and scientific foundations and only occasionally guided by the ordinary motivations of the ratiocentric ecology that has become mediatized, the one who is charged with making our daily menu, however honorable these motivations may be, since they feed the revolt against the tradition of cruelty and stupidity that subjects the animal to man and man to himself. In this sense, if it is indeed a fiction in the broad sense as we have always claimed, the fiction of a new life, it is certainly not an ecological style of fiction, enclosed within its disciplinary limits and its criteria, either scientific or philosophical, that should provide its relevance, but an ecology that we will not hesitate in calling a "utopia of combat," a thought more adventural [*aventurale*] than adventurous. It is about bringing the anxieties of ecological inhabitation to the level of thought or a life rather than that of some den politics.

Kant with Planck and Hilbert: The Transcendental of Superposition as Pure Reason and Solution to the Antinomy

However, this antinomy does not in itself provide the means for its solution, outside of the parties involved there will in fact have been no one to distribute roles and functions, no one other than themselves, than their forces and the abuse they create in the form of a trial, the arbitrary nature of which they refuse to see. Will there be someone to evaluate and transform their relationships? Maybe capitalism makes for something good to blame and even a good guilty party, but philosophy and ecology have so much affinity with capitalism that all three are compromised as false witnesses who skillfully manipulate charges and discharges to the point of confusing them. Their confusion could be worth a peace or a solution to a war that turns out to be a false conflict. This quotidian argument is, however, unworthy. Unworthy of who or what? Like all poorly engaged conflicts or vicious antinomies of this nature, this one comes from an abyssal contingency, and yet it is the honor of humanity, the only one, its own good and power, to want to establish principles of law in these conflicts and the rules for their solution. Obviously, at this point of aporia, if we seem to lack any perspective, it is because the definition has been partial or its position incomplete, it is impossible for a game to find a solution when it is strictly reduced to two positions, it lacks the magistrate, it shifts the conflict to his person in order to take charge of it. This judge or system of reference to whom we are appealing must enter the conflict, be part of the game, be relative to the two original opponents, at the same time as being able to judge the situation or "measure" it from his "relative" exteriority. However, in this problem, which could be called the "three body" problem in homage to physicists, and which involves the reciprocal relativity of all players, the third of which, if we can say that all players are relative in their judgment to each other, their relativity cannot be "general" in the sense that it would imply three numerically distinct terms. It is not certain that this problem of justice (within a philosophical game), once it excludes the transcendence of the divine Other or the theological solution, can then be resolved by an arithmetical deduction. The solution oscillates between an absolute contingency of terms that plunges all players into nothingness through an absolute hetero-referentiality, and what will be called elsewhere a semi-referentiality or a semi-relativity of the third term. Is it a word to disguise some ignorance, for example a transcendental solution in the rationalist sense of Kant? Or does its position and function distinguish it from the other two that form the antinomy?

Let us call this third term "Reason-in-person" or "'pure reason" or even the "Transcendental", though not exactly in Kant's sense, in order to distinguish it from its forms, for example rationalist and metaphysical ones that mix it with these contrary terms, with the experience it organizes. Reason-in-person is "pure" for reasons relating to the complex or imaginary number that abstract it from representation and, among other things, from Newtonian representation by means of an abstraction or what we will call a "lowering," to be explained later. Purity within the quantum can only come from vectors and their complexity, which is due to the pure imaginary number that begins its representation as transcendent.

This time it is a paradox of the philosophical which proposed an encounter with the transcendental, lowered or without transcendent support, and quantum physics in its principle of superposition. We raise conceptual paradoxes like those other ones with their "undulatory" cats before making them die, this paradox stipulates that there is an affinity between the principle of superposition as factum of quantum knowledge and the transcendental principle *once it has been delivered from its confusion with the apparatus of rational knowledge,* from its mixture with experience, with the subject, the *a priori*, reflections, its origin, or its Kantian meaning and its Newtonian basis. The transition to the quantum does not destroy the transcendental in any way, but only some of its functions and especially its tools, which Kant had transferred from "experience" or from the principle of the unity of experience. A single word defines it, it is "pure", even purer than the *a priori* that exists only under conditions of universality and necessity, therefore with reference to specific knowledge, but it is not "abstract" in the sense of transcendent. For the transcendental principle is the One that is *for* experience but is not derived from it, the One does not necessarily mix with experience. It does not even mix with itself as One-of-the-One, it is instead One-in-One as a superposition of the

One with itself, without analysis or synthesis. The pure transcendental or "in-person" is an intentionality that only aims transversely without thematizing them with contents that, strictly speaking, it does not fill itself with and on which it relies only to traverse them. It is a traveler without luggage or a vehicle, a wave without any support, the pure oscillation of an overlay or the universal form of knowledge, in other words its factum rather than its quantum. We will call this transcendental "Reason-in-person" or "pure reason," this is its formalism from the imaginary number or algebra, not even logical and so rid of the Kantian critical apparatus. Pure reason is obtained by subtraction, even that of the *a priori* always linked to particular knowledge such as constituted mathematics or quantum physics and the constants of this level which are transcendental semantic nuclei. The transcendental must be understood as an immanent One-in-One or superposed with itself and containing all the virtual power that it will deploy and distribute around it. There is a rationalist formalism of the *a priori*, that of Kant's, who withdrew from the empirical, but also another formalism, that of the superposition of quantum states, which has withdrawn from philosophical or "real" representation in order to take refuge in idempotence $1 + 1 = 1$, One-in-One = One. The same principle therefore functions at the upper limit of philosophy as a transcendental properly speaking, provided that it is discharged from its apparatus, open no longer to understanding and other means but to the universality of experience, and it functions as a superposition at the upper limit of the quantic, equally discharged from its quantum. An *a priori* apparatus and a vector apparatus do not specifically target the transcendental for understanding, it does so for itself and grants them this function, but they "technically" mediatize this destination according to the experience to be constituted as understanding. Under these conditions of abstraction, which make them pure principles, the superposition that comes from quantum physics and the transcendental that comes from philosophy are the two sources, the same source, of Reason-in-person, sources subject to a variability of their means as soon as they have to be put in the service of the understanding. The transcendental is lowered, lowered-over we will say, in relation to what traditionally supports it or carries it, the transcendence of philosophical representation. Superposition and the transcendental as it is modeled by it, causes Reason-in-person to sink into its own foundation, to become ruins, a foundation in ruins, to duplicate the surface on which it let us believe it was resting on, and to emerge from a leap into the open air of transcendence. However, it will be necessary to face the corrected evidence, even more so than at the opening of philosophical transcendence, it leaps into this openness promised by the quantum, Reason-in-person emerges from its ruins within the Universe as from a tunnel. In other words, this leap and tunnel from which it seems to project itself cannot in reality take it very far, less far in any case than philosophy can when left to the illusions of its spontaneity or its transcendence. The transcendence of the Universe is lowered-over compared to that of philosophy left to itself or to its desire for the absolute.

Affected or begun by the imaginary number characteristic of the quantum, Reason-in-person itself has two aspects, two sides that each group together all of the antinomy's content. Reason is first of all an external representation of the duality of these opposites grasped in their transcendence, but it grasps this antinomy from its own immanence to it, which is an immanence (to) itself, it is therefore also immanent to the antinomy in which it disseminates its own immanence. Reason-in-person is therefore doubly immanence, once (to) itself and a second time "to" the transcendence of the antinomy. This aspect or relationship of diffusion is the uni-laterality of pure reason, which is not isolated but shows itself or manifests itself within and through transcendence. It closes the antinomy from its own immanence without thereby enclosing itself completely with it, without mixing with its terms. Such a doubled function, interior and exterior to the antinomy, does not mean that immanence (to) and its diffusion are made by relation. It is the opposite, immanence (to) itself is what measures the exteriority of the antinomy as a residue. This double function of immanence is what is generally called the transcendental, but here its immanence (to) itself, its radical rather than absolute non-relativity or one based upon a transcendental term, determines rather than commands its exteriority, unlike what happens in philosophy, for example in Kant. But since this measuring by the third term or pure reason affects the other two equally in an immanent way and does not dominate them, we will say that it under-determines them or measures the relativity of each of the three terms, including its own. Its own? Reason-in-person, being immanent (to) itself meaning purely immanental, retains a certain transcendence but simple and not as a rationalist doublet. It is under-determined to be equal to all terms that seem to need to be moved to another region than the original or primitive one.

In reality, the system is even more complicated, because the unilateral action of the transcendental immanence (to) itself upon the transcendence of the antinomy is a double action, so we finally distinguish three layers and not only two: 1. immanence (to) itself or the essence of pure reason in which the two following strata participate; 2. the transcendence of the antinomy determined by this immanence (to) itself, in a way its most external material; 3. what this determination takes as a new duality from the antinomy and its transcendence, the new duality of the two parts of the antinomy that are this time like an *a priori* for the empirical content of the antinomy. These are the two *a priori* by which the immanence of pure reason diffuses into the empiricity of the antinomy and determines it. Let us distinguish on the one hand the old forms of reason deployed philosophically in a doublet as transcendent in an absolute sense, even when it is said to be transcendental as in Kant's case, and distinguish on the other hand the Reason-in-person which is without support or any "ether" to support it and relate it to experience, and which is stratified as we have said, 1. as a reason immanent (to) itself, 2. but also immanence "to" the experience which this time represents the transcendence of the empirical to which it must refer in order to under-determine it, 3. an operation that is carried out by the *a priori*'s duality. It is clear that Reason-in-person is constituted by the two opposing terms but which have changed in nature through the operation carried out by the essence of reason, they are no longer terms given by experience but are extracted by the pure and simple transcendental as the *a priori* that relate to experience.

It is time to highlight the scientific and "non"-theological meaning of this architecture of *Reason-in-person as it is given by the conjugation of philosophy with quantum physics, a conjugation capable of providing, through its immanence, a solution to the antinomy that philosophy forms with ecology*. The solution to the antinomy of philosophy and ecology is found therefore in its quantum "preparation" as access to the dimension of a Hilbertian "transcendental." The old Reason of rationalism is converted and transformed into Reason-in-person, and it is through the introduction of quantum means that its antinomy is shifted onto the terrain of science where it is solvable with a minimum of indispensable philosophy but without it becoming "fundamental" and dominant. Philosophy and ecology can only solve their antinomy if it is transformed or converted into a vectorial representation in the custody of the complex number, if we see in the antinomy two superposable states of thought rather than a dialectical contradiction. The solution's novelty is that of the superposition of addition of vectors by the force of its pure transcendental essence, the imaginary number is not mixed with experience but is "for" it retroactively. Reason-in-person operates with the terms of the antinomy as with two *a priori* that will combine to (under-)determine experience, but its transcendental essence is the simplicity of adding its vectors. The unmixed transcendental, "pure" in the abstract sense of Hilbert's vectors, not in the absolute sense of rationalist philosophy, is without a transcendent support to repeat it, it is not real in the sense of arithmetic but refers on the other hand to the transcendence of experience through the mediation of the *a priori* that it takes from it, and it is the quantum principle of the superposition of opposites or of states of the antinomy. It is an abstract representation, affected by the imaginary number and made by vectors.

A Messianic Ecology: The In-the-Last-Humanity

We are trying to build a messianitary [*messianitaire*] problem that will articulate philosophy and ecology through the mediation of a formalization of quantum provenance. There is nothing here concerning a new ecological treaty that lists in one great complaint the destruction of the earth, irresponsible behavior, exploitation, and abusive consumption. It is a question of raising vulgar ecology from its empiricist low-water mark and out of its litany, of making it almost speculative, theoretical instead, provided that human life lends itself to it and common intelligence can receive it. Unfortunately, it is not made for people who eat little by choice or by constraint, but less so for those who think little, who serve us and consume undercooked or poorly preprepared references.

There are other aspects of an ecological messianity or a life within the immanence of pure ecological Reason present as obvious issues. Man serves as a classical model for the animal that is still deficient, because philosophy continues to speak for the animal according to the man who serves as the animal's measure despite all his good will and repentance. It is one of the longest misunderstandings in history, if not a misinterpretation. If man was received as the image of God in the mirror of the world instead of in the mirror of the Universe, then how could the animal not have been taken as the dejected image of man even further distanced from the Universe? How can we rectify this hierarchy of images, this scale of downward specularity? It will certainly not be through a transcendent indivision of thing, concept, and essence, with the types of diversity that accompany it. No doubt we will have lost all notion of any human nature in the classical and metaphysical senses, but what can we replace it with? Not with a principle of continuity or continuous evolution but with a principle of the discretion of the lived for the living, including man, conjugated with a humanity that cannot be shared. It is a new principle of both matrix-esque unification or an egalitarian conjugation of the variables Man, Animal, Plant in the name of their unequal under-determination in-the-last-humanity. There is no human nature as a sufficient essence, only as a threshold or a quantum of humanity, a "Planck's humanity" below which no one can descend (against materialism), above which no one can rise or transcend (against philosophical sufficiency and metaphysics). A final distinction must therefore be maintained between man and animal, but it is no longer paradigmatic and humanistic, it is the distinction of generic man as before-priority or last-instance, and the priority that man and animal share alternatively within philosophy where they serve each other using heterogenous models and data (either metaphysical or physical). This is no longer human nature under philosophical precepts, but there is human nature such that physics can contribute, conjugated with philosophy, to its modeling. This limit is set immanently by the generic knowledge process itself and is not an external given. There is a problem of symmetry or invariance between humans and animals that incorporates both notions within science, with some adjustments or tweaking of the givens. But symmetry as positive invariance is broken with the introduction of generic difference that reestablishes its own symmetry or a generic invariance of-the-last-instance between living things despite all their differences. And it allows experimental verifications in the form of a genealogy of the lived (experiences) of animal or human appearances.

On the one hand, it is inevitable that we take on the essential aspects of the destruction of ancient notions of human nature carried out by the biological sciences or the scientific reduction of human beings. It is no less inevitable, on the other hand, not to forget the fundamental trait that has been misinterpreted by philosophy as human nature, meaning the small irreducible difference that makes up its function, neither its privilege nor its exception, namely that only man, man alone, has this altogether intelligible but somewhat uncertain power of being open to a scientific and generic constant of humanity that draws its measure from the Universe and in no way excludes human belonging to other "kingdoms" and their common problem of survival.

The consistency of the in-the-last-humanity requires it to be constituted as a fourfold of constants. From a generic perspective, life will be considered from a triple point of view, as a relatively autonomous and specific experience between the physics and psychology that borders it, as a real content in the form of a triad of living beings or genres of life (man, animal, plant), and finally as determined by a system of material and formal constants. The most important of those we will specify are the quantum of the lived rather than the molecular quantum, its imaginary number and vectoriell materiality, the procedure for indexing randomly produced subjects in superposition, and lastly the algebraic rule of idempotence that gives life its generic and "subjective" style. The first is that of a certain scientific rigor which is not the rigor of the human sciences, but of a new type of objectivation of common, philosophical, and even positive scientific statements, a new objectivation oriented by and for the in-the-last-humanity and modeled by the quantum. For a flaw in a rigorous and human form, a radical posture requires suspending all at once the cultural, linguistic, psychological, and even epistemological attempts to concentrate the system of the living ever more onto itself and multiple common performances and mixtures, affirming the sufficiency of the unity of life. We suggest we change the type of criteria and that we entrust this task of seeing an ultimate (but not philosophically sufficient) criterion to a generic theory inspired by physics, a distinction that will place the three principles (the protection of man, the animal's least suffering, the moderate use of the plant) under human responsibility of-the-last-instance. It is no longer a matter of creating a metaphysics of life, ether materialist or theological, but *a theory of the knowledge of life by itself*. The *a priori* and the constants of life more generally function as the constitution of an ecology-oriented discipline in a broad sense that goes beyond human concerns for economic survival and extends ecological care to the whole of nature and maybe—who knows?—to the Universe. The ideal of the forced humanization of nature, of the animal as well as man, verges on abandoning the otherwise universalist ethics of protection and the good sustainable and epistemological use of nature. However, under threat of a vicious ideological circle, we must keep as productive forces some of the means for taming life or its self-domestication, meaning that the "bath water" can always be used and we are never sure that we can keep it if we throw out the baby— meaning man—at the same time. It is urgent that we test with new principles the knowledge we are able to have about life and recenter ethics and epistemology on the "encounter," as we now say, with the animal and plants. This encounter calls for a new concept of MAP equality, a reevaluation of the notion of "human nature" and its degree of destruction. How are we to abandon or modify the metaphysical concept of nature so that we can ground these three principles at least? 1. that of safeguarding man as a safeguard of the in-the-last-humanity, man must be saved or protected, not exploited even for his own benefit, by virtue of his dignity adequate to the Universe or his complete non-belonging to the World, 2. that of the least suffering for the animal, the least suffering being all that can be asked or hoped for by the priority of the animal as Being-thrown-into-the-World, as well as that of man in so far as he shares this priority, the animal having no before-priority worthy of being safeguarded, 3. that of the moderate use of plants by virtue of their "insensible" nature and their Being-rooted-extatically-in-the-Earth, the plant can only hope for the form of respect that suits it, not to be exploited at will, meaning mobilized and made available as the animal traditionally is.

The problem is crucial, how do we combine the indivisibility of life with its discreetness? How can we take in the destruction of human nature carried out by the biological sciences, the radical inclusion of man within the equality of life, but not completely erase the fundamental trait that has been misinterpreted by philosophy as a separated human nature, meaning the very small irreducible distinction that forms its function of-the-last-instance? It is namely, again, man alone who has this completely intelligible power—however uncertain in its application to life—of being open to a scientific, generic, and minimal constant of humanity that in no way excludes human belonging in animal nature and their common problem of survival. The "in-the-last-humanity" requires us to constitute ourselves as a fourfold of constants specific to a discreet but unbreakable or indivisible humanity. In order to solve this paradox, we have to admit that life, far from being continuous growth, is marked by a general collapse or breakdown that the discretion of the quanta of the lived suggests.

Eco-fiction as the Gnosis of Ecology between Earth and Universe

Under-determination by the specifically quantum imaginary number is at the origin of a double work, two effects that together testify to human beings' ecological finitude, the impossibility of enclosing human being in a nature or an essence, in a dogmatic and reified, essentialized and thus determinist knowledge, and complementarily to this radical opening, not worldly but *cosmo-quantum* on the basis of the quantum giving form to theories and modeling an always open form of knowledge. The destination of man as the last-instance has as its correlate the transfinite invention of life, more than its "creation" (Nietzsche-Deleuze) which remains a theological concept. Humans do not only invent concepts, but they also invent theoretical fictions with bits of science and philosophy, and complexes like the Universe that serve as their parameter or measure. We are constantly inventing thoughts at the limit, transfinite, and vectoriell advances waiting to be confirmed, fixed, or summoned in a finite way. As the last-instance we participate in the Universe as a machine for making knowledge and hypotheses rather than for making gods, but as the last-instance we also manufacture them only on the condition that we under-determine them, meaning we leave them open, it is not a complete and determined knowledge, the problem is one of renewing them through superposition and quantification based upon their givens. As gnostic beings we are thrown into the Universe which is our being-thrown itself despite its tendency to constantly wrap itself in itself so as to enclose itself as World.

Eco-fiction prohibits a controlling and deterministic return to an *ecological life* marked and delimited, for example, by the opposition of Spinoza and Kant (Hegel included with him) concerning the problem of what is missing from a thing or of the excess it potentially can affirm. Or, in a completely different mode, to Bergson's critique of disorder in the name of creative evolution, which is nevertheless closer to messianic creation. What is missing within life or what is in excess to it? This question must be addressed by variables, a matrix, and the imaginary number, but not dialectically. A matrix of complex numbers captures the lack and affirmation (of positive ability [*puissance*]) as properties and then as variables decided retroactively, and from which generic man is posited as the subject distinct from them but capable of assuming them. They are canonically conjugated in the name of this generic subject, meaning in order to produce humanity as it will be capable, but randomly or probable as must be expected, of happiness satisfied with pleasure as well as with dissatisfaction, with positivity as well as with negativity. It is a generic and non-deterministic solution, the subject = X, that at the end of the oscillatory process of his probable production will be able to accept in its lived (experience) either the misfortune of consciousness and other forms of contemporary negativity, or both hedonistic ethics or what remains of them in the examples of Foucauldian pleasure or Deleuzian desire. In order to introduce the imaginary number into the lived as a circle of their opposition, or even more randomly within the circle of auto-affectivity as joy and pain, according to Michel Henry, perhaps it is necessary to introduce into philosophy, in an immanent and heteronomous way (which is only possible with the tools of the matrix and the complex number, not with those of philosophy) an operator other than the concept of negative magnitude [*grandeur*] so as to affect philosophy in an immanental way and in particular to under-determine it in a way that will not be entirely Kantian but algebraic and probable, a finitude as probability proper to pure reason but non-Kantian.

Quantum disempowering lowers the absolute or infinite power [*puissance*] of reaffirmation that corresponds quite perfectly to philosophy's double transcendence. It then becomes possible to confront what remains as simple affirmation, as Kant does with another operator, what he presents in a still classical style as "negative magnitude", or Heidegger as "non-essence" or *ungrund*, and to treat this duality of affects as non-commutative variables rather than as more or less circular philosophical affects. Disempowering must not be treated as a unique variable but in conjunction with human growth, with which it forms a matrix and complex duality, as a true quantum affectivity, and therefore random or probable but in no way deterministic. In their philosophical understanding of this affectivity, Spinoza and Deleuze have capitalism as their horizon, as might be expected, and in order to criticize it they take the risk of being too close to it. Affectivity, as well as knowledge, is instead here sought and obtained by adding obscure micro-affects that lack sensibility, random leaps from an affectivity punctuated by constructive and destructive phases. This type of oscillatory affectivity is opposed to the overpowering ontological proof of Spinoza and Deleuze, contrary to their redoubling between infinity and absolute, between perfection and absolute, even if locally it oscillates though circularly this time. If they are both philosophers of collision, they are both such in a Newtonian way, favoring an ontological joy that is carried within its intensity, erasing the sadness of nothingness and more generally the random character of auto-affectivity. It seems that like Marx and Nietzsche (and then Foucault/Deleuze in their extension of them), these philosophers confuse the microscopic order with a simple weakening of the macroscopic, they ignore the extent of the imaginary number's impact and develop a quantum without any rigorous decisive means, and so without real randomness. They can only reinforce the spontaneous political and ideological dogmatism of ecology by subjecting human life to the shackles of a metaphysics that disguises a mechanistic and Newtonian physics. To make human life possible, it is necessary to lead this absolute to degrowth without making degrowth a new absolute, without remaining within philosophy's absolute atmosphere. Its degrowth is as a result often lived as the degrowth of the financial or philosophical capital of the mind, as a continuous fall, a vague decline. We oppose it with a theoretically controlled degrowth that has an algebraic or immanent cause, meaning a quantum or a limit that testifies to the ecological self-knowledge of human beings and not simply to consciousness. Contemporary times are lived as times of decline, of capitalist dehumanization or other such forms as the demands of the new aspiring-masters take shape. Can we think, on the contrary, of "declinism" or of the bad infinite degrowth simply as a variant of amplitude in the manner of thinking and feeling such that it does not necessarily inspire hatred of the contemporary and so allows us to be the contemporary of our time from the point of view of affects or the lived? It is also necessary to lower in a grounded way the spontaneous philosophical pretension to "great" and especially "small" masters and events. How can we become a Stoic within history and capitalism, for example? It is a matter of placing undulatory and random positivity within this "quantum deconstruction" of the excess or even the collapse of philosophical power, especially since the negative and the positive no longer have their classical forms redoubled here to help us.

Following Spinoza, with the reservations formulated above against his idea of power [*puissance*], we distinguish between a non-philosophical *power of amplitude* and a philosophical Power [*pouvoir*], let us say between *potentia* and *potestas*. Even the lived experience of the surface as Deleuze explores it—apparently without double transcendence—must be understood more positively because the lived surface is still a simple transcendence non-thetic (of) itself that suffices for generic man if he does not satisfy the exceptions specific to *potestas*. This simple transcendence of the lived depends upon the initial conditions, it is a lived radicalization grounding an activity of resistance to *potestas*. The power (*potentia*) of the last-instance is a non-action and therefore an impoverishment [*abaissement*] of Power [*pouvoir*], an under-determination of *potestas*. Philosophy's *potestas* is due to its doublet nature and its disempowerment is its lowering through the power [*puissance*] of the last-instance. Philosophy's power [*puissance*] is the sufficiency of acting as well as reacting or the reaffirmation of acting, it is Power, its power is generally principal sufficiency. The reduction of this *potestas* as sufficiency is not therefore necessarily opposed to *potentia* which is a causal form of reduced *potestas,* it being one of its modalities. Degrowth of God's transcendence and the absolute, in and through generic immanence resulting from the collapse, is a kind of under-determined knowledge rather than a fixed and axiomatic kind. In order to produce an effect of generic degrowth, a cause as radically under-determining collapse is necessary, its radicality signifying that it shares causality with the intervention of philosophy.

2

PHILOSOPHY'S DEGROWTH FOR A GENERIC ECOLOGY

Ecological Times

At another time we called this problem: "struggle and utopia at the end times of philosophy." Obviously an anti-Hegelian formula, not all thinking is determined by the philosophy assumed to give history its sense. The "end" is not the end of philosophy but of "the times," it is not an intra-historical, still philosophical event. The "end times" is an eschatological formula, the context is that of humanity of-the-last-instance or of the in-the-last-humanity. This is the new use of struggle and utopia, of a philosophy finally made available to humans. What can its function yet be in times of ecological distress, when ecological finitude replaces metaphysical finitude?

It is not a question of the philosophy of degrowth being addressed here and there, but of the degrowth of philosophy itself. Non-Philosophy's most visible effect is the reduction of philosophy to both the state of an object and the materials of production for a science specially called "generic", which is no longer a philosophy of the positive sciences. Philosophy is only a productive force to be put in the service of humans. We argue that it is not yet that and has only been such in a rather reserved and perverse way. We are not saying that it is an ideology, it is a productive force that has been turned into reproduction.

"Philosophical Horror"

In order to prepare us, here are some scandalous statements falling under a heading that should merit some nuance . . . "Man is the most terrible Being" (Heidegger); "man is a wolf to man" (Hobbes); "man is a living monstrosity" (a neurobiologist). And yet, "the philosopher is man *par excellence*" (the philosophers). This set of statements will be called the symptom of the non-separability of man and animal. What is this non-separability which immediately avoids deciding what man is within what is usually called "man" and what the animal is within the animal? Now we are in a state of great uncertainty regarding the determination of these two entities. Philosophical horror lies in these always possible arguments, but also in philosophy's ambiguity.

Philosophy is the first model [*idéal*] of overgrowth before all the others, the one that legitimizes the others if it does not produce them. There is a misunderstanding about its aims, to increase the virtues or the good, to decrease evil, this is perfect, but philosophical humanism also adapts to this causality called domestication, breeding, taming, and the passage from the pre-human or inhuman to the human, which is the content of a realist and deterministic ethics, that regarding which we have to ask ourselves if it is really made for the human race. Alongside the virtues that are its humanist and moderate version, there are the transcendentals and their categorical vocation, and even higher is the Platonic ideal of the more-of-philosophy, of the philosopher's more-of-joy, and it is true that philosophy is an object of extraordinary enjoyment [*jouissance*], sometimes it contains examples of Foucauldian pleasure and sometimes of Deleuzian desire. There is also the right to philosophy (Nietzsche, Derrida), the duty to philosophize, finally the immanent auto-justification of philosophy. To philosophize is to justify philosophy, to ensure the full use of its will without having to measure it against an exteriority that would not be a semblance.

Philosophical Models of Degrowth

Do we have to oppose, and for what reason, the philosophical models of degrowth against philosophical inflation? Deflation? Occam's razor? Less philosophy? Its deconstruction? Another weaker practice of it, as some Italian philosophers want? More multiple, like Deleuze? Or its economic marginalization, its final nihilism? Or, on the contrary, should it be even stronger, always strong, like Badiou? These solutions suffer from a vicious sickness, they are ultimately continuistic and only recognize a vague *philo-diversity*, finally naturalistic and almost without any radical scientific principle to speak of, philosophy's specular invariant, these solutions prolong philosophy's auto-sufficiency and homogeneity, assuming philosophy will transform itself through the means of these solutions.

We pose the problem in another way, by combining philosophy with a more radical and truly heterogenous means—that of science— within it and outside of it rather than with an otherness that is either vague or theological for the moderns, can we continue to use philosophy? The science of language already demonstrates that *philosophy has the structure of a double articulation*, at two levels, which brings it closer to language, that it forms a spectrum to be analyzed and explained as a structure as doublets or as a double transcendence, that it is driven by a certain "Principle of Sufficient Philosophy" which is the superior level and the unity of meaning that transforms dualities into doublets. By reducing it to a global thought, to a single level with degrees, cases, or nuances, the solutions evoked *overwhelm it with a positivity of a scientific type as if on a mirror without really using science.* So that for philosophy, science does not think spontaneously, because to think we would have to speak, and philosophy furthermore uses science to simply reflect on itself.

Non-Philosophy is Not a Downward Speculation

Evidently it is not a question of imposing a simple degrowth upon it, and quantitatively, continuous in this case, what exactly would degrow? Such a degrowth of knowledge, of art, of philosophy, of science, of religion would be at odds with philosophical degrowth but it would in fact be the same auto-philosophical model understood this time as a conservative and regressive reaction. On the contrary, *generic degrowth proposes to reduce philosophy to the state of a productive force*, so that only the principle of Philosophical Sufficiency has to be removed. And for this task, we need an appropriate science.

Philosophy is a speculation floating both upwards and downwards. But this is its self-description, as if the wave were described by the sailor tossed on this wave (see Leibniz and Kant). Another nostalgia, land-based rather than marine, philosophy only thinks of growing like the Cartesian tree or, according to Heidegger, sinking like roots into the ground. Or it projects itself into a great living thing. We take seriously these aquatic, vegetable, and vital metaphors of thought bearing witness to ecological nostalgia. But non-philosophy does not simply describe fluctuations or oscillations without explaining them, receiving them as affects, being content to endure and live through them. It is a matter of understanding philosophy's undulations, ebbing, and surges by applying the science of undulations (particles and waves through vectors in a space of configuration or of imaginary numbers). A science for philosophy must respond to specific constraints, not only on the same plane as its object, but this object (very special because it is philosophy) is never manipulated by a simple and brute science. To avoid this simple face-to-face confrontation and war between different kinds of knowledge and thought, it is necessary to invent an apparatus imposing upon them a "perpetual peace," a conjugation apparatus for two disciplines that preserves their autonomy or specificity while depriving them of their desire for principal domination, getting rid of their respective principle of sufficiency linked to philosophical spontaneity and to the positivity of scientific domains. Hence a preparation against their immediate use, in order to bring them by force to the negotiating table and create a common or generic space. This negotiating table is what we call the "generic matrix." We are not at all pretending to propose a "general ecology" but simply a generic one, this is exactly the contribution that we can make as those living in an environment of philosophical origin without limiting ourselves to an everyday ecology. Let us not waste philosophy on "down-to-earth" tasks as a substitute for theology.

An Ecology in the Quantum Spirit

For philosophy to become an object or an ecological concern, it is therefore necessary to meet a certain number of conditions, to invent their implementation, to create, to put it all out there, an adequate theoretical "installation." We cannot continuously transfer the problems and means of ecological thinking directly to philosophy, we need new definitions of proximity and risks, new divisions of knowledge, and to settle on related objectives.

The Paradox of Productive Forces of Degrowth

We place the quantum and philosophy together in a chessboard-like matrix as non-separables, having a common interest or meaning for nature, in order to re-examine each of them within this situation from the standpoint of human subjects. It is not a question of potentiating them in an apparently reciprocal way, of seeking a meta-science or meta-conjugation of forms of knowledge. On the contrary, we would like to free ourselves from the vice of these knowledges that rooted us in the world under philosophy's authority. This is non-philosophy's object and not only a brute and positivist scientific degrowth of the concept.

The process is apparently a ruse since we multiply one form of knowledge by another as if we were increasing their power. But on the one hand, they are no longer disciplinary forms of knowledge placed separately in their transcendence, their spontaneity, and under their own principle of sufficiency, *their disciplinary knowledges are now simple states or properties of a human subject = X that they do not directly determine*. And on the other hand, these forms of knowledge deprived by this quantum-inspired vectorial apparatus of their respective principle of sufficiency, are not organized by the imaginary number that is the quantum secret and then indexed to this dimension that is called "transcendental" or "universe," which is the second quantum structure. The multiplication of non-commutative properties produces the paradoxical effect of a generic degrowth of knowledges oriented by and for the subject = X. This is instead an extension and an activation, a subjective repetition of the quantum degrowth of determinism and realism, an aggravation of this movement by placing these properties at the service of man as subject = X. *The generic matrix solves this ecological paradox regarding productive forces that can be forces with an effect of degrowth or de-productivity*. How can we produce degrowth instead of always producing overgrowth? Generic science cannot therefore be a general meta-science but an "under-science" or a "hypo-science."

From Linguistic Doublets to Quantum Dualities

So we are moving from a linguistic interpretation or one that comes from language to a physical and quantum interpretation of philosophy that better respects certain distinctions of philosophy and grounds a well thought-out degrowth. A quantum analysis (supplemented by a generic orientation) is substituted for the language-based model that favors the logocentric auto-erasure of dualities. This proposed degrowth would be dangerous or irrational if it were interpreted within the framework of linguistic presuppositions. But physicist reduction is not physicalist and naturalist, it does not lead to primary representations but to dynamic conceptual experiences. For the still massively philosophical model of Lacan and Derrida we substitute an analysis according to an onto-vectoriell model rather than a simply vectorial one, ontological rather than a geometrical model although using the under-basis of geometry. If the double articulation and the doublets that make it happen tend to erase themselves in a linguistic practice that does not go beyond auto-philosophy and limits deconstruction to auto-deconstruction, then there is a completely different possible duality, a quantum one, that of the wave and the corpuscle in the form of the vector and the particle. Even if it seems to imitate the signifier and the signified, which is the lower layer of the double articulation, it is more scientific and algebraic and does not risk falling back into logocentrism because the vectors are no longer oppositional, negative, and relative (Saussure) but can be represented in an imaginary space called the configuration determined algebraically according to the imaginary number (square root of -1). And moreover, the model of the corpuscle and then the particle makes it possible to subsume all the forms of the signified and of meaning. As for the upper layer of the double articulation, that of discourse and unities of meaning, it too will be transformed and will lose its theological and fetishistic virtues of enveloping dualities. In concrete terms, the double articulation of philosophical discourse will be under-determined, meaning it will lose, in accordance with the quantum model, its layered identities and those of hierarchical relation, of sufficient unity that forms its philosophical kind of singularity and universality, in order to take on an indeterminacy and a non-localization, for example a signifying non-opposition, in relation to a subject called "generic." The sequencing of philosophical discourse by itself, despite everything in Lacan and Derrida, will be prohibited because it would be a false degrowth of philosophy.

However, the endeavor does not stop there, it is also reducing metaphysics for the benefit of the generic subject. There is a subject of this degrowth and it is no longer the philosophical subject, it only undergoes the degrowth by implementing it, undoubtedly, but in a relation of causality called "in-the-last-instance." Degrowth as a theoretical and generic concept, not as economico-political doxa, is therefore based upon what could be called a scientific practice, in any case, but also through a distant reference to a "generic Marxism." It does not describe a situation in the concrete world or a phenomenological anthropology of man in the world, it is a theory of philosophical action within ecology, an action that is more probable than certain and more aleatory than dogmatic.

An Ecology in the Gnostic Spirit: The Epistemic Natural Environment from the World to the Universe

We are proposing to change ecology's ultimate reference environment and to answer a little differently the question of nature and environment. The quantum model requires us to argue that the correlate of quantum physics, and not traditional *physis,* is the Universe and not the World. By Universe we mean the correlate of modern forms of knowledge guided by quantum theory and by World we mean the correlate of philosophy, the Universe not being the great mystical whole of certain physicists but an epistemological correlate of physico-mathematical knowledge. The Universe, even as an object of experimentation— especially if it is an object of experimentation—that thinks itself, is an object of knowledge and not a material object. Once this has been established, the reference to forms of knowledge must be distinguished from the reference to the World and find the Universe as its true correlate, such is the consequence of this gnosis. Despite these generalities, our objective is very limited compared to the field of ecology and its Platonic presuppositions, even if gnosis is partially a result of Platonism. Contemporary human beings inhabit a world of knowledges that proliferate rather than a world of sensible objects marked by theology and therefore by sin in the old way. We therefore suggest an extension of the ecological domain, man must be prepared to transgress the natural World and to enter the Universe as a theoretical object and not only into the World as a biological environment. Ecological or generic finitude cannot exactly replace the old finitude of subjects, its sphere of sensible and cognitive existence has expanded in its materiality and within its formal possibilities by renouncing the mirages of totality and the absolute. According to this modernized gnostic context, we will say that man has generally fallen into the World as evil or nothingness and that his problem is one of fleeing this world because, in a less religious way, he is thrown-and-measured-by-knowledge, meaning thrown into and measured by the Universe, on the basis of various knowledges. His problem is not one of finding the universal environment as an original ante-predicative that he would have lost, but of defending himself from the confusion of the World and the Universe by using knowledges against their philosophical capture. The ecological problem is being shifted to that of the best non-worldly use of the world, and therefore of the epistemic natural environment. A particular distinction is required concerning the place of philosophy, which is both knowledge among other kinds of knowledge and a productive force, and the world-form *par excellence* that diverts knowledge from its universe-oriented use.

This positioning of the problem does not imply a worldization, but a naturalization of the episteme. If there is a capital-world, it is that of the knowledges, but can we reclaim these knowledges without their world-form? The paradox by extension of the procedure adopted here is to treat philosophy, which usually gives these knowledges their meaning and their truth, as the material of a knowledge in order to finally rid it of its relationship of duplication to itself and closure of itself. Knowledge, including the most ambitious thinking, must be treated as a natural ecumene, an inhabited surface of the earth's crust and subjected to its collapse, but more extensive, more universal, with supplementary dimensions, than its former relationship that was circular in reality and closed to *physis*. *It is universe-oriented rather than world-oriented*, there is an intention of these knowledges, it is the Universe, just as the world is the intention and a "noema" of consciousness or of Being. It is a matter of naturalizing philosophy in the strong sense of modern physics rather than of *physis,* without using Quine but instead using Marx and Planck.

The generic extension of humans into the Universe is not a continuous or even infinite extension of the World as Husserl would have it. We have moved from the World to the Universe, from worldly ecology to universe ecology through what can be called the true "quantum leap." Thought is not the intrinsic property of humans and this should be used to define their essence (as we would gladly call it in this "local" case), it is a halfway uni-versal that must be freed from the "anthropic principle." If we push forward animality to bring it into culture, as happens today, why not push the highest humanity in order to bring it into the Universe and, by a paradoxical example, re-examine anew the costs of its link with animality, to see if it too is worthy of the Universe? Let us suppose an ecology of relations of thought, of the highest forms of it we can make use of, science and philosophy, art and religion, relations with and within the Universe that we again specify here is not the great mystical whole but the intertwined correlate of these knowledges.

The Imaginary Number and the Raising of the One as Macroscopic Sufficiency

The spirit of non-philosophy or non-standard philosophy is the One, but this thesis has been misunderstood. It is not about the One as metaphysics or the duplicity of the One-of-the-One, but as radical immanence of the One-in-One which does not designate anything other than the quantum superposition or Reason-in-person. This is a new "non-ontology," the representation of variables, i.e. those of the quantum and philosophy through vectors as imposed by the imaginary number used in quantum physics, vectors that form a new duality with philosophical representation but not a duplicity. This is a reversal of the One proper to the superstructure within the One-in-One as an *infra-*structure composed of vectors. The imaginary number has a general effect of subtraction or lowering-over or even an onto-vectoriell under-determination of those knowledges subtracted from philosophical representation. In other words, the One as a factor of unity or identity, eventually duplicitous, is suspended, apparently a little like the unity-of-the-count Badiou speaks about, but the imaginary number only suspends the One of sufficiency or makes it immanent without getting rid of it in a materialist way. It weakens the worldly sufficiency of these knowledges, that of the encyclopedia in general, including philosophical knowledge since its own sufficiency is not only the positive naivety of science but is twice sufficient, once as direct, first, or principal, and a second time as vectorielly or indirectly.

Now philosophy and quantum physics no longer collide in their sufficient or macroscopic spontaneity but are two simple properties or predicates for a subject = X. Refusing to presuppose the two is the principle of the sufficiency of these knowledges which believe themselves unique. Our own rational kernel is no longer dialectical but physical and quantum. So what we need to raise is not the One in general and the unity of the count within its abstraction, but *the One-as-sufficiency*. In the One-in-One we seek the formula of a contemporary gnosis as a superposition of vectors capable of weakening the World's hold, which is made in the form of knowledges when they are over-determined by philosophy. This is not the sort of "bad" imagination that grows and nourishes a philosophy without rigor and therefore denies it the possibility of a philo-fiction, to the contrary, the imaginary or complex number is a productive force of the degrowth of metaphysics. It is an amputation of philosophical excess with a directly positive effect, a positivity of withdrawal-without-retraction or the subtracted-without-subtraction. Onto-vectoriell immanence under-determines philosophical growth or over-determination so that degrowth or under-determination is not an ontology of lack or the negative to which the full and affirmative ontology of Spinoza, Nietzsche, Bergson, and Deleuze could immediately be opposed to. It is a vectoriell affirmation without reaffirmation, but the absence of a second affirmation does not destroy any selection here, on the contrary. Philosophy is here "degrowth-oriented."

The One-in-One is now a form of the unconscious or the infra-structure, the impossible real, if one wants, or that which does not fit into the philosophical order, but there is no question of eliminating it or killing it as Badiou says. Because it will emerge with the philosophical superstructure and its doublets, but under its own authority of the imaginary number or vector indexed to itself as "last instance." Standard quantum physics (helps to make) non-standard philosophy, it does not project itself specularly into philosophy but transforms it. Quantum and then generic under-determination as Last-Instance is a general lowering of disciplines to the state of vectoriell properties, and transcendental and absolute principles to the state of objective or immanental appearances.

It means abandoning the processes of Lacanianism and deconstruction which is a complex and Judaic-oriented Lacanianism. Philo-fiction is a genre parallel to science-fiction, a lowering of philosophical dogmatics and axiomatics to the state of fiction. This is placed between the real and objective reality and allows them to be joined together without mediation. Philosophical dogmatics suffocated the truth between experience and objectivity. It is about loosening the vice that encircled truth.

The Productive Forces of Degrowth (Epistemological Reductions)

Science and philosophy are theoretical productive forces that can be used in theoretical *pragmateia*. There is a use of scientific positivity included in a practice of understanding, this does not mean that we treat them as if they are only practices but that we treat them here uniquely as productive forces that do not have their end in themselves, but within them and outside of them, that is for human beings as ecological subjects. When science and philosophy are "naturalized" by quantum modeling they are no longer models outside the order of knowledges or metaphysical paradigms of thought and life, but "simple" forms of knowledge used as productive forces for a transformed species of knowledge that can be called "truth." It is curious to announce an extension of productive forces with some degrowth in mind, but in realty the naive use of science and philosophy under their respective principles is the source of all excessive use as abuse, and their reduction to a state of forces is the best way to consciously place them in the service of human beings. It is true that this reduction is implied for and by the construction of the matrix that already presupposes this reduction otherwise deprived of meaning. The matrix is alone concrete or real here, the "disciplinary" sciences or philosophy as a paradigm are no longer the concrete.

Subjective Ecology of the First and the Last Instance

How are human beings ecological subjects? The metaphysical dissociation of man and animal is rejected as too simple and macroscopic. We work, as always in the quantum spirit, from non-separable dualities. First that of animals and humans, their non-separability or their non-locality will be posited in various possible versions. We then distinguish between the first objective the before-first objective or that of-the-last-instance, both of which deal with this animal-man non-separability. The immediate and primary goal of ordinary ecology is preserving the natural environment of existence, or even preserving man and his survival as a species, but we distinguish a goal that is before-first or of-the-last-instance, still man-animal but in its power to under-determine the primary goals. In the "defense" and maintenance of human environments, spontaneous and naturalistic ecology must be arranged as a defense of generic man in and sometimes against the environment of knowledges. It cannot be said that this new objective for ecology is superior or meta-ecological, it is a *generic use* in-the-last-instance of epistemic environments, the best appropriation of the forms of knowledge (including philosophy itself) with the defense of human beings against their drive for self-destruction in mind. *A distinction is made between the philosophical ecology of human animals which live in-World and the ecology of human animals that live generically in-man and so with the Universe in view, between the protection of the environment and the defense in-the-last-instance of human beings*. Hence the subordination of philosophy's great classical objectives, even of truth, moral conception, and the metaphysical elevation of human beings to their ultimate horizon, this being their ultimate safeguard in-the-last-instance against violence, including ecological violence.

Degrowth: An Only Probable Imperative of Non-Philosophical Ecology

Consequently, the degrowth of the forms of knowledge as they are driven by philosophy. It is a matter of grounding ecology on a non-Aristotelian but also non-Newtonian basis. We refuse the philosophically sufficient and its naturalism (rational animal or creature), we must change the terrain epistemologically at least, suspend the world or nature as idealized metaphysically, meaning the determinism that goes with it and the realism that allows anti-animal violence. But after causalist determinism has been eliminated through the quantum, we have to regain generic ground or point of view, both quantum or matrix-like and indexed to man as a generic subject dedicated to the practice of eco-fiction since this is an ecology in-the-last-instance and not a physics.

1   As it always affects a moving duality, which is philosophy, generic degrowth cannot be a quantitative but a qualitative question and must be helped by philosophy itself as its occasion, it assumes an analysis of philosophical complexity, a quantum apparatus which is that of a probabilistic knowledge of this special object, philosophy. The degrowth of

philosophical sufficiency is based upon the understanding rather than on disciplinary practices of breeding or domestication or even macroscopic transformation.

2 Generic man requires an experimental kind of understanding and not a mechanically deterministic and substantial deduction. In accordance with the quantum spirit, two states of the generic object must be distinguished, its real state named "aleatory subject" obtained from virtual possibilities (non-philosophy as "prepared philosophy") and its indexed state as a clone in the dimension of the Universe, a state named "in-the-last-humanity" and given as the final measure of human beings. The uncertainty of understanding only concerns the experimental understanding that take human beings as a set of probable subjects and not as philosophers. This is not an immediate understanding, at the level of its premises, but a vicious ideological confusion. It only appears with the repetition of the experiment or the "second measurement" as physicists say, instead of immediately with empirical or aprioristic givens. If it has a limited or under-determined "*a priori*" aspect, it is so not as first but as "before-first" or as preparation for the conditions of understanding. Probable understanding that commands only with uncertainty, with probability because generic man is not the object of an absolute and axiomatic definition, he is known through his properties which are variables, he is an observable object before being an observed object. This cannot therefore be about a continuous degrowth of transcendence generally, non-philosophical ecology is a "prepared" or aleatory ecology.

3 There are negative ecologies in the sense of "negative theologies" but the under-determination of transcendence is a positive operation of selection within philosophy rather than an exclusion from it. It is an effect of an operation of preemption or the removal of a layer of transcendence, the most human one, as it results from unilateral causality or what we will call the clone. Preserving the vectoriell part of transcendence that defines human generosity is the effect of a positive act that no longer aspires to an over-transcendence as philosophy does, but to a "under-transcendence" that has suffered a "collapse." It is a mistake to understand negatively the notions of the *a priori* defense of man and degrowth.

4   For all these reasons, which are effects of generic man and not only as a species facing others under the generalities of animal and reason, or as a reigning and dominant species, the principle of Ecological Sufficiency will be refused and we will conclude on a probabilistic ecology based upon the principle of uncertainty and the production of "clones." Ecological sufficiency, or even anti-ecological sufficiency, results in absolute or ideological decisions in one sense or another (such as the refusal to train and consume animals) that are supposed to be simply natural (whether in-man or outside-of-man). This also presupposes that man can freely and all-powerfully decide to safeguard or destroy nature, whereas he does not quite have the power to transform it from top to bottom since he belongs to it in each decision, to include and disrupt nature, to put it into play as in any new decision. He just has the power to under-determine his decisions. We will need to reflect on the non-separability of man and animal, and on the animal both as model for the positive science of man and as clone of man.

3

THE HOUSE OF PHILOSOPHY IS IN RUINS

As philosophers participate in life and not only in Being, they also inhabit a House, a main dwelling body that is always too small, requiring immense outbuildings be added to it that are always too vast, the World or the Universe. They too, like their inhabitants, know this collision chamber, its wall and its breach, the everyday collision of its inhabitants, they have their quick-tempered or peaceful way of leaving this place. For its part, the Cave, which the philosophers modestly began with, finds its response in the modern house's cellar where the bombarded take refuge, from either the sun's fiery rays or the flashes of explosions. In both cases, we must be able to climb up to the open air of deliverance and into the great opening of the Good and of Peace.

Philosophers present themselves as the rightful or first occupants of this House, though they do not yet know is in danger of ruin. The greatest and most "well-off" claim to be showing it to future occupants who are invited to "see the place" and who know that they will always remain tenants on some small scale. Philosophers are real estate agents for large open spaces and small enclosed spaces. As part of this task they have a problem to solve, and it is often a problem of space, great effects are expected from means of modest space. The house is a spatial and ecological paradox, the model of the smallest human habitat. It is a philosophy in miniature, philosophy itself is a building too small for what it would like to put inside of it, to unfold nebulae, to compile an inventory of stars, angels, and theological populations. The sky would not be enough. How, for example, can we accommodate a world where complexity alone is universal, put it within reach of people who think little about the narrow perspectives that landlords judge impossible to honor and respect the places that they claim? Humans are sometimes like the eating-little subjects of ecology and sometimes like the thinking-little subjects of philosophy, they occupy a rare and unmeasurable space that falls neither into the very large nor into the very small such that they never stop being around each other.

Let us finish the paradox, we will have to place or grasp the house in a state of ruins to fill this space of common ownership and identify those who inhabit these ruins. This will require a bridge stretched over this abyss and its being hidden from the frightened eyes of philosophers, a means to fill this in-between that has neither been found nor built by them, to ensure the suture of two infinities that mark its boundary. If we now bring together these architectural and organizational conditions, the increased enclosure and openness, collisions and bombardments, rarity and ruins, the conjugation of the World and the Universe, the two infinities, a single thought makes it possible to build this bridge, a single apparatus fulfilling these functions, this is the model of fusing the quantum and philosophy.[1] It will be the quantum modeling of this dwelling as an ecological "thought experiment." If, moreover, one wonders who, what living being, can fulfill these conditions of a universal ecology for all forms of life as they are lived-without-life and as abstract from the living, we will move toward the only ones capable of passing from the state of the living to the state that will be called generic clones, bypassing any biological conception of cloning. The inhabitants of the House of Philosophy are called clones as the *blind with their eyes wide open* to the approaches of the aleatory shores between a small infinity and a big infinity. First, we will describe the House of Philosophy in its ruin, reserving the description of clones for the end of this essay, inserting the descriptions of the procedures followed for this metamorphosis into the interval between these other two descriptions.

A dwelling is a philosophy materialized in miniatures, whether it is a skyscraper, "madness," or a country house. Even the simple shelter or the cardboard box of the poorest people changes the concept of housing, makes it uncomfortable or lays the sleeper out in a different way under the sky, but does not destroy the concept. Bring into the house its articulation and distribution of parts with instruments of passage, corridors, doorways, stairs, elevators. The house is not some transcendence in general, the empty space of a height under which one is forced by different means to hold itself together. We distinguish classically, that is to say comfortably, at least two floors or a ground floor and first floor, this difference in classification will be important for understanding the practical use of this instrument. As a philosophy in miniature, the first floor above the ground floor corresponds to the raising of experience toward the universal, Kantian *a priori*, or Platonic Idea, it is always necessary to go up even if this staircase is replaced by a corridor, because the expenditure of energy required to make use of the corridor confirms that there is always a rise even when it would only be toward the bottom of the corridor and the rooms at the bottom, meaning toward the inner horizon of the house which is only a plane locally and abstractly. The second staircase fulfills a very different function than the first in that it hopes to put an end to the fatigue of the first and provides hope for some final success. Although it was built in the wake of the first, it tends to merge with its end and leads to the highest point, a ridge or skylight in the roof, or a watchtower for a prison or concentration camp from where one is free to catch sight of the panorama of the World which concentrates all directions, so sometimes literally concentration camp like. This point is the absolute of the second transcendence, it is the One, the end of real transcendence. After the One, there is only dream or despair, re-descending toward the initial doorway with the satisfaction of accomplished work. This is the house that we, as philosophers, live in with naivety and common sense—a doorway that is at best always already stepped over, the double staircase of transcendence, the last leap into the One, the Good, Moral Law, or the Absolute as a reduplication of the One, and finally the fall or triumphal return to experience.

Now, let's change our perspective. We have described the house as an object within a horizon with an external view and an internal view that connect through the doorway. Let us assume that this cave is not doubled [redoublée] at the same level as our stairs, but it is divided [dédoublée], not another cave behind a first cave but two intertwined caves that no longer connect except through random and unpredictable trajectories. We will encounter some difficulty getting out of this underground system to the doorway of the interior of the house, emerging into the open-air rooms of transcendence. In reality, it is unlikely that we will leave the same way we entered. For, from this new point of view, everything changes while remaining the same. What is this "all," this geometrical, this figure of the house subject to metamorphosis? The rooms and their passageways, the articulated content of the house continues to impose their topography and routes. And yet we only see and experience the house from this interior, which was symmetrical from the outside. This splitting of the cave or cellar produces a catastrophe within perception or rather within the perceived. Instead of summing up the redoubled identity of the house and transforming the perception of it as a property dealer [marchand de biens] would do, the splitting of the cave makes it cross from bottom to the top of horizon, in a way the water line that horizontally cuts the house in two (it simplifies or reduces this identity) flattens the relief of its composition but not in another dimension. What is this de-doubling of the cave but the introduction — instead of the unique and transcendent cellar of the Platonic cave which is any room with imaginary or hallucinatory depths — of a cave now split whose structures are quantum, square root of -1, the effects fractured and thrown like particles colliding on the black screen. It pulls each room to itself, shares it or cuts it through its fault and thus fills itself with particulate objects, and no longer corpuscular ones. Plato inverted!

The famous Cave was therefore only a screen capturing traces of light like a wall capturing shadows, the descent of Heraclitian fire fulfilling itself quantumly. The "top" rooms were apparently corpuscles that also inhabited transcendence and never stopped repeating themselves specularly in the form of vestibules, antechambers, boudoirs, back rooms, etc. But when they are affected by the quantum sun (freed from the yoke of the Good), the split is that of an invisible black whose spark fills the screen.

Even more profoundly than this vision, which already definitively abandons the viewpoint of the watchtower on the house's articulated content, the catastrophe takes on an apocalyptic dimension, literally "in relief," a hollow relief. Ruins spread out like pieces on a chessboard, spreading the wave that occupies the whole space, it is still a copied transfer of representation, a flattening of the house. But an immanent upheaval now affects the entire building and the ruin of the interior of the quantum cave or collapse. What happens to transcendence, especially the first staircase? Finding a foothold and being rooted in the quantum cave, it no longer starts above the doorway but below it, integrating the doorway by passing it and rising from the Cave or collapse from where it started, toward the rooms on the ground floor or at least as we have seen, from their lower part which it cuts out and upon which it "gives" directly. The first transcendence now takes root more deeply than its apparent deployment. This is a metamorphosis, a spreading of the staircase, more than ever you seem to be walking through an endless corridor but you keep going up, it is the ruin of the staircase as if it falls endlessly into itself. Without destroying it in its invariant nature as a staircase, this metamorphosis spreads it out or extends it infinitely as a universal staircase that will never stop climbing without leading to any "big room" that can be located in terms of functionality—a dining room, a bedroom, playroom—but to their indivisible entanglement. The House of Philosophy is beginning to be uninhabitable like a schizophrenic house, its half-closed or half-opened rooms seem to be made for disjointed, partial, or even particulate individuals, perhaps giant Lilliputians.

What happens now to the upper staircase and the watchtower that it emerges into, such that it blends in with it? Its essence is that of any staircase, the jump from one step to the other, the partial jump of the endless path and the absolute final jump. That the absolute is given again at the end of a final ecstatic leap is the properly philosophical essence of philosophy, its double ecstasy, that of Objects or Ideas, and then that of the Good or the Real, before it sinks into the mystical or into the pure matter of the real. The leap with which philosophy forces itself up from the bottom of the Cave remains unthinkable or as simply given for philosophy, the same is true for the jump at the end, philosophy is unable to think of the two jumps that frame its life except by making a circle of the two, an impossible repetition of the imaginary number. As for the watchtower, like a bulwark that the panoptic gaze onto the World carries, it is also beyond the World and covers in a single glance its panorama but also, if it turns around to cast a look backwards, somehow over the shoulder of the world, then for a brief moment the infinity of the stars in the unique depth of the sky can be seen. The House of Philosophy closes the world and, locking it up, opens it up on its inverse side as a universe and undoubtedly on the in-verse as Uni-verse, as immanence of absolute exteriority. This is precisely the complexity of the jump from the tower, which allows us to glimpse the difference between the World and the Universe. Before it was the small difference between heaven and earth that was enough for the philosophers, after it was matter or mysticism. The watchtower allows for a double view: the one that encloses the World on itself and the one that opens it on to an absolute exteriority. This double function is necessary to define philosophy's double function, even if it is an unequal relationship, the first function is dominant and repressive of the second, or the inverse. These two asymmetrical instances contained in an identity make up all philosophy.

But the tower is also affected by a catastrophe that spreads its two instances and equalizes them in the algebraic form of an idempotence which expresses the identity of the tower with itself and with each of its two moments: World = Universe, therefore quantumly through superposition World + Universe = World *or* Universe. The identity of the House of Philosophy, when it ceases to be seen externally as an object with two specular faces back to back, is now reduced, seen in an immanent way, carried out as a true identity that is said of each of the two faces and their duality, as an identity that resorbs its exteriority like a glove that finally adapts to the immanent form of the hand.

It all began in the very depths of the Cave where philosophy slept dogmatically. It required a seismic distance from itself, which puts it behind and ahead of itself through the imaginary number, a collapse that hollows out a chasm into which the house soon falls. This transformation was prolonged by the changes that affected the double staircase, spreading it endlessly like a corridor that must be climbed without knowing that it is being pulled to pieces. The stairs also fell into ruin and then the tower in turn crashed into itself as a flat identity.

This is the ruined palace that Kant speaks of without daring to go to the end of its description or its destruction, until the ruin of its inhabitants, a ruin that gives rise to "boundless admiration." He always evokes them between the cave or the mine and the sky "above" them, torn between the stars and the moral law, this is the double philosophical viewpoint of the tower. Rationalism only has a macroscopic Newtonian form, poorly worked out, for the quantum in the form of debris or stones "scattered on the plain of experience" like after some atomization or air disaster, a *flash becoming a crash*. Rationalism only grasps debris from the House of Philosophy as if it has been vitrified, rather than as a true quantum partialization. It knows only nuclear fire, which is the misuse of the quantum capable of simply and without delay ruining the palace that philosophy would have been.

What is finally coming to pass, assuming wrongly without a doubt that philosophy supports a "final solution" to the point of being a terrorist solution? The somewhat pretentious edifice of this palace of mirages "falls into ruin." Everything must be read here. It falls because it implodes from the inside, or even in an immanent manner, like those skyscrapers that are made to collapse onto themselves in a cloud of Humean dust to the great delight of those children of television that we are. The affect of absolute ruin, fear, and joy may not be for us. Precisely because the House of Philosophy only falls "into ruin" by conserving itself in those ruins, keeping part of its functions and its figure as a virtual or dreamed image grasped from the distance. This crushing onto and within itself, which conserves the form of the new weakened thing, is called collapse (co-lapse). Let us summarize the state of the situation after quantization using the three strata of the *Critique of Pure Reason* to help us. Intuition, the foundation of the building, is ruined as a particulate unconscious of the Cave. The stairs of transcendence, meaning the forms of categorical objectivity intended to reach and configure the object, are ruined or pass into the state of ascending vectors, endless, and capable only of partialized or fractured objects, those of the floors and the ground floor. Finally, the difference of the tower collapses on itself as a simple identity of idempotence. This was the House of Philosophy's concentrated point from where we dreamed of the World as "Universe" and the Universe itself as the infinite that borders the world beyond its horizon. Its falling into ruin through the collapse desutures the World and the Universe in order to render them non-separable in a new form by way of this non-substantial link of entanglement, which is the quantum as the essence of the Universe. This is philosophy's role as a form of the World, to expanding itself to the whole Universe and to solder together the ruins, to rebuild the house. This is how the House of Philosophy once again offers its ruins to the Universe as a spectacle worthy of human tragedy.

4

THE ANTINOMY OF ECOLOGY AND PHILOSOPHY

The Antinomy and the Urgency of its Solution

If ecology tries to claim a legitimacy mainly in the face of philosophy, between ideology, politics, and positive science, then is it not necessary to seek the instruments of justice so as to make it a rigorous thought, to elaborate their new relationships which are also the relationships of humans with the earth and with life? It is a new antinomy which emerges, which is still not very noticeable, and a "new" ecology that is less dependent on empirically copying the living, including human beings, and locking them in a positivist circle. Ecology is for the moment, despite its technical and political efforts, a low, massively ideological, and media-based form of philosophy and wisdom, which it is detached from and with which it is gradually entering into a rivalry with. As for philosophy and its theological foundations, which have sculpted man as a creature belonging to the kingdom of "nature" with other living things, there is an eco-logical form, specifically Greek, one cannot deny it, and a more modern form, specifically therapeutic. It is true that "great" philosophy, and its most speculative principles, does not have the daily well-being of these living things (so namely men, animals, and plants, as well as the well-being and conservation of the earth) as its most obvious function. Philosophy is content to cast a severe and compassionate glance, a look of domination and a glimpse over the earth that it struggles to again descend to—but has it ever descended there for the first time, if not in the speculative form of some materialist position? Philosophy does not yet know that we only go down to Earth from below. The philosopher, when he cares for the living or takes care of concrete life, does so in a distant style of theological origin, a priestly style, and in the macroscopic concern for large groups, he claims to be a doctor for large bodies, of the State, of the soul, of civilization, sometimes of sick or wounded bodies. The auto-therapeutic use of the ego, language, society, and humanity able to move toward a cure or some "taking care" of life, is a long tradition that is consubstantial to it but often turns into a self-medicating, which ecology contains an equivalent of. We will summarize these problems, being those of antinomy but broader and more relaxed than those of the rationalists, by saying that there remains a large, increasingly visible gap, a Platonic chôra between the ends proper to philosophy and the scientific means available to human beings to protect or destroy themselves, a gap that incurs costs of mixing, encroachment, abuse, failure, and laborious negotiations between these ends and these means of heterogeneous origins.

Here the objective would put an end to these mimetic rivalries where an invasive ecology gains ground over philosophy and shifts their relationships without denying one or the other so as to establish new relationships by introducing into this struggle recent scientific forms of formalization and conceptualization that would distribute rivalries differently. In distant memory of Kant, we will seek a new court or magistrate, a tribunal of reason to judge this dispute rather than this conflict with less heteronomy or Newtonian exteriority. Without returning to a rationalist and critical solution, a tribunal is necessary within and for reason itself, that means *a science that immanently affects philosophical Reason and is likely to make ecology the foundation of a new "life" better adapted to human beings*. Only Quantum Reason, engaged here in an exercise that is little found in its current positive and scientific practice, can force us to recognize a principle of a radically immanent auto-limitation of philosophical access to the real of life. This auto-limitation assumes as a priority philosophy's reduction, no longer only by itself but guided and pushed along by quantum algebra and the imaginary number, which alone can detach us from this immediate belief that we will try to extend from common representation to philosophy, and make us admit the necessity for this to pass from the living to their being lived-without-life. A delicate mission of infiltration, the imaginary number will in particular allow us to avoid going back through the faculty of the transcendental imagination and repeating the Kantian and Newtonian tradition of classical physics in favor of a more contemporary and universal tradition, as well as helping us avoid the positive Darwinian version of living things. It is a matter of accessing a fully human "ecological life," an eco-fiction if you will, and one articulated through nonempirical disciplines. One of our assumptions is that the quantum will be able to assume a more universal renewal of ecology and that, without drastically eliminating philosophy entirely, it will be able to make room for it, to include it in a broader system combining an "ecology in the quantum spirit," on the one hand, and the old ecology of the philosophical tradition, on the other. The solution consists first of all in making the quantum and philosophy two variables related to the core of the lived-without-life, thus reducing their antinomy to two non-commutative properties, it is the only way to break with the mixtures and confusions that disturb the simple philosophical organization of life. This "generic" rather than "general" ecology, and the "lived" rather than "life" will fulfill the ends of philosophy with the means of the quantum once transformed and included under the sign of the "in-the-last-humanity." It will not mark the "end of philosophy" as some hasty thinkers once said with all seriousness [*sans rire*], but "the end of philosophical times at the birth and foundation of an ecological life."

To get out of the current situation, which, as always, testifies to the beginnings of a new discipline of philosophical domination and not to a scientific treatment of the problem, we will therefore transform the two conflicting theoretical environments into conjugated variables in order to radicalize the situation in a rigorous way through its extremes. The philosophical side as one of the variables will gather together in its name all the forces of inertia, repetition, and resistance to invention and discovery that are liable to be philosophized, while the other variable will see the substitution of Newtonian thinking (being ultimately that of positive ecological sciences but still under a philosophical organization) by quantum thinking capable of refounding by means of a certain formalization and modeling the productive scientific forces of a new ecology that is capable of enveloping philosophy. This shift will affect philosophy and ecology, redistributing their components and causality in a different way.

It is no longer a question of fashioning a vaguely hermeneutical philosophy in order to bring the existing ecological sciences up to speed in terms of their assumed meaning and purpose. Positive ecological sciences do not have to be surpassed or transcended by philosophy, that would be to return to an old domination and the bestowing of meaning, but they must be transformed by their companionship with philosophy into a common quantum matrix that will conjugate them. This solution of the conjugation of variables avoids making this double transformation a problem of schematism, suture, or bridge building between particularly heterogenous scientific and philosophical extremes, with the recourse to a unity of synthesis by the imagination. The shift in the relationship between ecology and philosophy requires the introduction of a non-Newtonian and non-Kantian science, a scientific means that is an under-determination capable of fashioning an expanded ecology embodied within philosophy at the same time as ecology envelops philosophy. This science operating through immanent under-determination of the two disciplines contrasts with the old Kantian schematism of over-determination or synthesis made by the imagination and which relates the original unity of apperception to the forms of intuition. However, there is indeed a process, it is vectoriell and complex, which by a power of subtraction affects philosophy, this is the square root of -1 or quarter turn (Lacan). The vector is the imagination but in its subtractive work operating on the representative forms of philosophy and breaking their circularity. Since there are two variables and not only one, there must be a complexification of the traditional schematism of pure reason and not only of complex Hilbertian vectors. This schematism lowers or, as we say, "lowers-over" philosophical transcendence by rooting it in the difference or subtractive withdrawal of the quarter turn. It is for this reason that the knot of the quantum and philosophy with its two variables reduced to vectors, form two universally non-commutative products, both projects conjugating their power of subtractive schematization. If we take into account the two variables determining the subject = X, they are products of vectors and not linear schemes of Kantian and Newtonian origin. Quantum noncommutativity is more universal and of a different kind than the rationalist and linear scheme or the transcendental imagination that it loosens, and that still marks out a theory of faculties, and limits itself to one of the products and not to the whole canonical conjugation of the variables, meaning vectors. Vector figuration renders more complex the schematizing figuration of rationalism between idealism and empiricism.

The Forces Present in the Antinomy's Solution

Let us follow very approximately the Spinozist duality of power (*potentia*) and Power (*potestas*), but by giving new content to both. Let us set apart an action that is neither pure nor infinite, not even a *re*-action, a *re*-acting in a circle of reciprocity, but a true transfinite action, so not quite Spinoza's power, the essence of which envelops existence. The ontological proof does not apply here to the quantum field and must be eliminated as the bad infinite and actual power of all-philosophy for a transfinite action. We assume it is lowered or lowered-over to the generic or radical rather than raised to the absolute of the absolute. For Spinoza, the being-affected of power at least in the attributes and the modes serve it as a correlate, power is the possibility of being affected. But how can infinite power and unilaterality be combined? Is there anything exterior that affects infinite power? We reject the Spinozist and Deleuzian model of self-affecting cause of itself, because quantum decoherence or microscopic duality does not fit into this unitary logic. The logic of vectoriell-imaginary causality that we oppose it to assumes a solicitation or motivation according to its duality of micro/macro structure when it would only be such in order to be "prepared" for the experiment. However, it cannot be said that the wave action re-acts to the occasion, even if the occasion that motivates is part of the apparatus and is such along with the system prepared for the experiment. The two form an indivisible whole but not a circle of reciprocity. The affirmative and re-affirmative power (Nietzsche) proper to philosophy is transferred into the mode of the self-cause, while the power of the quantum-generic last-instance that follows is an almost quasi-transcendental superposition with even less of a subject than the self-cause but capable of generating a probable subject. The essence of vectoriell action is not auto-position or self-cause but wave superposition in its algebraic nature of complex vectors. Conversely, the *potestas*, which philosophy exploits, is a complementary reaction and a factor of objective appearance. From this point on, we can distinguish the gestures of philosophical relaunch and quantum preparation. The relaunch as a typically philosophical reaffirmation has a spontaneously decoherent effect (first as a vicious circle of action/reaction, this is an act of *potestas* or Power), while the quantum preparation proposes itself as an under-determining or breaking of the vicious circle. One of the consequences of this mutation is that the wave power acts secretly, it is a non-action whose paths cannot be grasped any more than can the trajectories of a wave action can be grasped. In this sense, we can say that the interfering action is a non-action or a non-visible, waiting to produce a randomly visible subject. Finally, philosophy and the quantum are contrasted according to their fundamental concepts as power and Power, as determination in-the-last-instance and self-cause, as quantum preparation and philosophical reaffirmation.

The New Ecological Science

The problems of the antinomy are linked to the duality of philosophy, to the multiple dualities it manipulates and to the types of their cuts. It cannot be said that philosophy ignores this structure as dualities characteristic of the quantum, but only that philosophy treats them as more or less specular doublets and so therefore under a transcendental and/or absolute unity, as reversible. There are two analyses of philosophy, a self-analysis that is essentially entrusted to transcendence, with some efforts to exceed it with a whole practice of reaffirmation (Deleuze, Derrida, Levinas, Badiou), and then there is a hetero-analysis entrusted to the immanence of quantum physics. In other words, a quantum deconstruction, about which we have to wonder if it is not the real deconstruction in relation to deconstruction's philosophical form which hastens to rebuild with stones and debris, as Kant said, the old building instead of letting it fall into a state of ruin, and which, because of its method, is not rigorous and makes sacrifices to morality and religion. Moreover, are not the famous superimposed quantum states tower blocks or palaces, macroscopic corpuscles set to ruin by the force of this instrument, the imaginary number, square root of -1?

The problem is the ambiguity of the considered syntactic structure, in both cases it is a unity that is either reversible or unilateral, but always the One and the Two together. The *potestas* of philosophy as principle of sufficiency is a doublet of transcendence for both the first and second time. Within the quantum, the infrastructure/superstructure is also like one and two but not in the same way as philosophical transcendence. The generic matrix as *infra/super*-structure and the philosophical decision are very similar, except that the latter is realized as simplified transcendence or a finally circular auto-transcendence, whereas the latter is distributed as a developed process of knowledge since one passes from the philosophical circle to its quantum spreading as a duality of the real object and the object of knowledge. The structure of the One/Two where the One is just as good as the Two is found in both solutions but not in the same form and relationship owing in this case to the quantum as vectorialization and its operation of addition. Vectorialization initiates the process of knowledge because the wave and particle sphere of superposition already contains all possible vectors as potentials, some of which will then be actualized as products of knowledge after the "reduction of the wave packet."

What is called the new ecological science therefore derives from a different distribution of theoretical structures present, the quantum and philosophy as they intervene by way of their own conflict and deep within the more attenuated conflict of ecology and philosophy. They can be opposed in a simple way as a quantum vectoriell ascender based on the imaginary number and as a redoubled philosophical transcender, as the ascender of the module arrow targeting a particle and as the macroscopic transcendence that repeats itself or reflects itself in the corpuscle. Vectorialization is a cut in the relationship between immanence and transcendence, the latter reigning more or less alone in philosophy, whereas from now on it is immanence as vectoriell and simple that (under-)determines the double type of philosophical transcendence and makes it appear as a phenomenon of the superstructure. It is an attempt to focus thinking on the act of throwing and rection, on this operation that is completed but not closed. While philosophy is a closed or enclosed thought, a finitude that imitates the infinite circle of the whole and is enclosed without it, physico-quantum finitude is the rection or transfinite amplitude of the open. Vectoriell description is the effective degrowth of philosophy against its sufficient auto-description because it reveals philosophy's auto-dissimulated duality. The rigorous cutting of the vectoriell infrastructure explains the genealogy of this philosophy, but does not exactly cut again across the intra-philosophical doublets. We understanding why philosophy is always double in order to finally deny itself as such, we are no longer content to simply observe and practice it, nor even to "reduce" [« *rabaisser* »] it by placing it at the level of vectoriell immanence, this is a therapy for philosophical overpower, a way to heal it by leading it to a certain degrowth. So, it is explained that the overpowering or overpotentialization of thought is a permanent excess compared to what humankind can do, a way of growing dangerously. Human reason's misfortune is that of wanting to go beyond its generic conditions. An immanent cause of this degrowth is necessary, it cannot be stated in an ideological or decision-making manner as an imperative, there is no imperative of degrowth, an imperative is always in a state of excess as we have seen in the discourse of democratic opinion that is almost always self-contradictory. Degrowth is violence against philosophers, an injury and a humiliation, worse than nihilism that can always be relieved and recaptured, whereas there is barely any way to fight against degrowth since it is not a dialectical movement. So, is this a withering away of philosophy like the Marxist withering away of the State? Less of the State and less of philosophy, a general deregulation of thought rather than a market regulation of philosophical opinions? We are looking for a regulated solution, explaining the necessity of a degrowth that is not a renewal of philosophy, but is related to a measure or norm as a constant integrating its under-determined or uncertain being, a probable and not dogmatic degrowth, not an imperative or just a generic imperative, meaning a human one. What we often call a lowered transcendence.

This cut that redistributes and complicates the material is a new line of demarcation operating within the very transcendence between cause and effect. Let's try to sketch this out in two examples. Deleuze practices the reticular, bilateral, and infinite difference, philosophy's auto-description or that of the One-All. He moves to the Spinozist equilibrium of the Möbius strip through successive inversions. Deleuze's secret is the exact overlap of immanence and transcendence, of subtraction and addition within the Möbius strip while we retain their difference, like in Marx between *infra-* and *super-*structure, but in the very precise form of unilaterality, which is what the transition to the vectoriell plane allows for. The generic matrix conserves the immanence/transcendence difference as a unilateral duality whose two components no longer overlap as before, it conserves unilaterality at all costs, as long as possible, as an immanent duality or a last-instance. There is indeed a generic doubling of the imaginary number but it is not itself specular because it is through superposition. Here addition is the cause of the unilateral cut, it is necessary to add a vector to the previous one in order to obtain a cut or subtractive vectoriality.

Deleuze presupposes the One-All as a body-without-organs, or at least virtually as such, and this is achieved or sufficient transcendence, whereas we only presuppose the last-instance or the before-first flux and the occasional cause in relation to the vectoriell cause, which cannot be taken from sufficient transcendence. The last-instance is not a totalizing unity taken from the transcendence constituted, it is an immanental instance and not a transcendental one. The vectoriell analysis is based on this kind of unilateral cut, on the distinction between an ascending but immanent vector or immanence by ascending, and the philosophical transcendence of the in-itself. What counts is not consciousness or the for-itself, but the spontaneity of a transcending that is more than "originary." The cause is immanent but through ascendency or modulating and it is not an infinite univocity, but an immanent spontaneity and transfinite in the mode of the wave or state vector. It seems that the unilateral as transfinite is the dividing line between transcendental philosophers and immanental ones. Therefore, as a generic matrix it is a combination of unilateral syntax and the physical real or imaginary number.

Badiou also practices philosophical auto-description but as subtractive through the Cantorian set or multiple. Ontology is then folded back onto sets, cut between subtractive ontology and a meta-ontology that is part of philosophy. It is a cut or an abrupt unilaterality by subtracting the void from philosophy, hence an almost negative, private, ascetic style, especially in its beginnings as a subtraction from the void or the infinite, it is a negative dogmatics. Hence the question, how can the void act on representation itself in order to free itself from it or to subtract itself from it? Is it not a magical or authoritarian act of Sartre's kind of "for-itself" where the for-itself is held by the empty set, this being the decision for a mathematician Sartre? A decision in the absence of an experimental process?

A Transcendental Science of the Lived-without-Life as Knowledge (of) Itself

The problematic framework will therefore be that of life under the species of the lived-without-life, and not that which is too narrow and has become specular or vicious for man and animal, especially since it is necessary to add the plant as well and then consider this triad of living things. In order to open up this attempt in its ecological dimensions, so terrestrial and perhaps cosmological, we will try in a phenomenological but quantum spirit to treat the lived as, on the one hand, an indivisible experience, a lived-without-life, affirming its relative autonomy and the specificity of its phenomenon as an environment of existence specific to living things. To undo its immediate confusion with physics and psychology, with materialism and psychologism. Lived-without-life is distinct from the matter and psyche of the human sciences that it nevertheless borrows from, this is its relativity. But also to record the echo of the quantum principle as a quantum of the discrete lived. We hypothesize that knowledge about life is real but fundamentally unstable and that it can be known, even if in a probable but rigorous way, in a modeling effort that comes from physics. And, secondly, we hypothesize that it is undoubtedly *partially intelligible because of the intervention of man as a principle of-the-last-instance or as a generic factor*.

Without a doubt, when it comes to life we are particularly condemned to oscillate between science and philosophy when not between physics and psychology, so as to have access to a layer of lived and rigorous experience and to accede to its phenomenon. Human intervention, less in physics, more than in psychology, is always decisive but equivocal and subject to hasty decisions. Darwin and Bergson are the two great thinkers of the essence of life in a way that conjugates science and philosophy. Darwin also has philosophical means at his disposal, as Bergson has scientific means as well. But this fusion of otherwise differential and continuous means remains under the domination of philosophy or within a philosophical orientation, either materialist or spiritualist, and barely penetrates into the phenomenal and indivisible specificity of life. On the other hand, Marx is a great generic thinker, rather than a philosophical one, and orients everything differently than Darwin's and Bergson's knowledge of life. Our thesis is apparently paradoxical, man is undoubtedly an ordinary animal and at the same time, perhaps not quite at the same time, he is the factor that requires life, in order for life to become thinkable in its relative separation from physics and psychology at the same time that he has recourse to both of them in a relationship — called "entanglement" (in the quantum sense of the word) — of the probable subject and the objective form of knowledge or superposition. The generic is neither pure or positive physics or psychology. The generic is the human or anthropic principle, certainly not anthropo-logical, that gives a new amplitude to modeling, a limitation also of the use of positive physics and psychology as well as limiting their philosophical interpretation.

The struggle against reductionism or the physical or psychological over-interpretation of life is difficult to assess. Because physics and psychology are not to be totally evacuated they can be used as modelings and not as reductions of life and its intelligence. On the one hand, life borrows the modeling of the problem from physics (instead of from positive biologies) in the weak and reduced form of its knowledge and refuses to get lost in positivity. We will remember Schrödinger who tried to extend quantum physics into biology.

Moreover, life borrows from a psychological modeling as regards its object or its ontology this time, we will soon see this with the quantum of the lived. Aristotle and Bergson will be evoked here, but in a less spiritualist way. Finally, we will evoke Marx who understood in a generic way this autonomy of life, man as a natural being who makes nature human. Especially in his early writings, he sometimes tries to link the physical and the psychological together within the generic human. We will also do this, though with nuances that relate to the introduction of vectors and the imaginary number. The physico-psychological synthesis takes place in the subjects of life, meaning the three types of living things which are the three stases or modalities of life, the living as types or forms *a posteriori* of the experience of life.

Once the sufficiency of these philosophical interpretations of life has been rejected, how can a theory that moves to the conjugation of science and philosophy in a seemingly similar but completely different way be justified? In any case, we need a scientific interpretation, here it is the quantum that is the most operative because it allows us to integrate and limit the philosophy of life as a variable, which suspends the various interpretations in terms of the all-philosophical and makes possible a generic interpretation of the matrix. Hence a double movement with regard to philosophy: its suspension by way of its reduction to the state of a variable and so its relative conservation as a given or dimension of life; 2. its substitution by the generic which brings this science back to the humanity of-the-last-instance, meaning without humanism.

Since physics and psychology are required here not as sites of experimentations but as possible modelings of the science of life, how do they work? Quantum modeling requires a form of Heisenberg's "quantum principle," a discrete constant that can be altogether enlarged beyond the quantum physics of action, but which remains specific to life. As regards its psychological modeling, it requires that this quantum of life be a quantum of the lived, and so indivisible and discreet. The lived is not an ordinary general environment, an auto-encompassing generality, it distinguishes itself through its constant which is discreet and specific. This is an environment for the system of the three living things and at the same time by virtue of its discreteness it is not encompassing in the sense of the philosophical whole. This antinomy is the very antinomy of the quantum, both indivisible and discrete. We enter the sphere of life through the lived, which is no more reduced to the psyche than it is to nature. The lived is to be understood as an objective entity drawn by the imaginary number from the psychological but irreducible to it. It is the substance of life, even with the plant, the "lived experience of consciousness" (Husserl and phenomenologies) being only its transcendent(al) and irreal restriction. The constant is here an epistemological and transcendental tool, not a substance, it instead defines a relatively accessible sphere of phenomena for a constraining scientific attitude. This quantum of the lived signifies that we do not seek the *Being* or *consciousness* of life, but its *last or its before-first humanity*, we do not immediately tack on an ontology to life, whether it be a Darwinian evolutionary materialism or a Bergsonian spiritualism. Philosophical ontology will be well included and used in the generic matrix, counted as a necessary but reduced variable or one without sufficiency.

But why look for a physical plane? It is less a question of a modeling of life in its ontic specificity than a modeling of the knowledge of life in its genericity. Without reaching self-consciousness or being a pure positive exteriority, the human living thing is defined by a certain knowledge (of) itself, although the lived is not the generic itself as it will depend on the algebra of idempotence in the form of the "in-the-last-humanity" as we will see in that case.

Ecology's Matrix and Vectoriell Transplantation

Man = X is a real object to be determined in the form of a generic lived subject whose experience of his knowledge is prepared from a catalog of possible givens, axioms, and virtual properties that we grasp in the context of a matrix at a given moment from the various knowledges or from what we call ecological spontanism. These properties belong to a well-known double register, they are definitions that come from philosophy (the animal as rational, political, linguistic, believing, etc.). But to prepare man for this experience of ecological understanding, we use a quantum apparatus instead of a philosophical hermeneutic, this is not a matter of rereading or a reinterpretation of the humanist statements of philosophy, but their extension and their generalization (generic, nonstandard) through the means of a collider of two knowledges, one of which is philosophical and the other itself quantum. On the philosophical side, we give ourselves two predicates as materials torn from their classical representation or even their formulas-definitions, the immediate unity of nature and man (Marx), or Being-in-the-world, or intentionality (Husserl and Heidegger). We are not doing exegesis or hermeneutics, we take them up through their behavior, which is that of axioms that will serve as variables in this apparatus. Each of these formulas and their entirety are determined from the point of view of their exact meaning by the philosophical context of their extraction, but our theoretical context is no longer philosophy alone, and each of them is now, as a state vector, indeterminate from the perspective of this apparatus, they are for us virtual observables or potentialities rather than axioms. This is not a problem because their old kind of objectivity, which is philosophical, is subjected to a formalism still unknown to it, a new theoretical apparatus that combines so-called "complex" vectors, they will function as variables of the equation determinate of the generic human = X. It seems incomprehensible to consider them in this way, as pure theoretical behaviors rather than as semantic contents to be elucidated, but it is the fact and the work of this formalism that must resolve the incompatible nature of these statements by bringing them into a new homogenous epistemological sphere. These formulas have an original philosophical being but a different theoretical position that transforms their original being. As much as Marxism distinguishes in its structural way between the Being-of-class and the position-of-class, this apparatus of the vectoriell matrix distinguishes the spontaneous philosophical or ecological origin and the quantum behavior of the statements. Reducing this information to the state of superposed vectors, this is what we know *a priori* of potentialities to be actualized, although unpredictable, as generic man = X. The fact of using them as variables is an act resulting from a physical and naturalist modeling, but we do not stop there, these variables will allow us to pass from natural and/or metaphysical knowledge to physical and then generic knowledge, which is our objective.

The axioms-statements are treated as if they were addition-able vectors that only deploy in a Hilbert space. These vectors can be added or these statements superposed but only as complex vectors, which does not mean identifying themselves (an impossible task) within a single concept or object (on the basis of which of their elements, signifiers, signifieds, meanings?). Superposition is not an identification, but an addition of vectors with summation and resulting during their addition, and it applies to both phenomena of signified and signifier. This "vectoriell" interpretation is possible if generic man is associated with an imaginary number that under-determines him and allows statements to be treated as abstract vectors. We cannot think the unity of the definitions of generic man, because, for example, they would talk both about man, matter, rationality, etc. We must move on to another level of objectivity that is more formal but which is not inevitably going to be the Kantian transcendental like a rationalist instance of unity. This passage will instead be carried out through an indexing to an immanental superposition that is the dimension of the universe, in order to understand that generic man supports these two definitions without being transcendent philosophical unity.

Therefore, the generic matrix does not simply treat each statement as a positive vectoriell phenomenon, both as undulatory-lived and particulate. It treats them retroactively as properties that serve to define this subject. However, these vectors as properties multiple one by the other (in order to "close" or at least "center" the generic enclosure on man or on a last instance, even if it must remain indeterminate because of Heisenberg's relationships of uncertainty). The order of their multiplication is not indifferent. By virtue of the principle of indeterminacy, their inverted products are non-commutative and cannot be attributed together to generic man as a unity or identity of self-recovery of some same object. Generic man is known in a random or probable way at the end of the process either as an animal or as a rational thing, or even, depending upon what is initially given, as a vector of phenomenological Being-in-the-World, or as a vector of either a feminine or masculine sexuation, but never as a predictable unity of an object. The vectorialization of intentionality or of Being-in-the-World is the algebraic and generic reduction of these "wave packets" or clusters of interfering state vectors which are superposed states offered to philosophers as an appearance of transcendent phenomenological simplicity. The same algebraic and generic reduction applies to the physical and sensible man of Feuerbach and the young Marx.

Let us try to imagine what the result of this is for noetico-noematic intentionality if it is only a vector. It is an act that does not close or end in itself, but is only relayed by an object that is no longer an object in-itself but a noema. Indeed the arrow of intention meets an object but it can always surpass it, the noema. The noetico-noematic "correlation" is unilateralized, it is a unilation without reciprocal or overlapping relationships, the wave-particle association without reciprocation of the intentional arrow and the noematic particle. Under these conditions, the phenomenological axiom of philosophy becomes a non-phenomenological axiom of the quantum and escapes the closure of the world. Phenomenology is re-treated as quantum but without this being a matter of two predicates relating to the "same" subject, there is no longer such a unitary subject. Unilateral duality or complementarity makes it possible to overcome correlationism as a reversible generality (or "co"), the dialectic, materialism, and all absolute positions. To recapture materiality as the real content of the young Marx's "logical materialism" in favor of algebraic materiality or material formalism.

Cloning or the Indexing of Ecology to the Universe: Clones of the In-the-Last-Humanity

A new supplementary principle of unification is needed, a new dimension of the system of the living within the matrix itself, in the form of a second introduction of man as probable subject capable of "knowing" himself in-the-last-instance within life and beyond his animal life. This is no longer a transplant into the soil of the matrix. What does man have to do here, when he is not yet produced or manifested quantumly as an aleatory subject? Isn't it a vicious circle? This introduction is no longer that of one of the variables, of man participating in first animality, but that of the before-first man as the carrier of philosophy and quantum algebra, indexed to the Universe as to the very dimension of superposition, and so acting retroactively on the MAP system that is first and treated by the matrix. Man is one of the variables but he is also the carrier of the algebraic logos, fusing with the superposition that replaces the One of sufficiency. It is now the idempotent One that binds Man to the Universe, the superposition of which is the testimony of it in life, in the same way that this treatise is the testimony of the Universe's presence at work in philosophy. This suspension of the One of sufficiency has revealed a residue formed of dualities of states specific to the living thus prepared for processing within the matrix. But we must preserve a certain privilege for man and instead admit his immanent duplication, his intervention at the extremes of the process, first as a probable subject and then as Being-of-superposition or clone indexed to it. But this duplication is not an ontological hierarchy, it is simply operative, the possibility of thinking and objectifying by under-determining its initial situation within the biological circle. It is to struggle against the philosophical principle of anthropological sufficiency, which applies to everything and anything, with the *anthropic of-the-last-instance principle* which applies to human clones and this in-the-last-humanity without returning to theology. However, it is also necessary to *respect* theology and to not practice a *tabula rasa*, which is only possible in mathematics and not possible in physics. Man's privilege as before-first through redoubling is fundamental without being a philosophical nature or essence. The suspension of philosophy or of its sufficiency reveals a matrix ontology of the lived and not a set-theoretical one. In other words, Heisenberg's "quantum formulation" *([pa . . . ap]hi) where i represents the transition to complex vectoriality for both variables, and where h represents Planck's constant*, would only apply for matrix physics and not yet for the generic dimension which is an inclined fusion of the quantum formulation in the sense of the dimension of idempotence. Heisenberg's formula is sufficient and complete for the generic only if we perhaps accept that the human represents not just algebraic logos as a complex number but also the minimal quantum from which there is the lived-without-life. It is necessary to posit more than their synthesis, their idempotence which makes them generic. *This idempotence of the imaginary number and the lived-without-life is no longer called "man" or "human" and still less "animal," but "clone" or even the "in-the-last-humanity."* The in-the-last-humanity is the empire of clones that testifies to the presence of the Universe within humanity and life. The lived constant must be idempotent for there to be the generic and for man to distinguish himself slightly from the animal. The lived is Planck's constant which applies to the living reduced to their common lived experience, but generic man, the obviously non-biological clone, is the constant of humanity, of the in-the-last-humanity, and he is yet another thing that opens ecological thought to the Universe. *By grounding non-standard ecology on the axis that joins the Clone as lived-without-life to the Universe, it seems to be based upon two incommensurable and non-commutative entities, but this is precisely their idempotence and not their synthesis that must solve this problem*.

In biological knowledge itself, MAP are ontological and epistemological models of each other in different senses (M as paradigm, A as provider of givens, P as possible metaphor for M) and allow us to understand each other relatively through one another. But they are not yet variables of the lived that can be multiplied one by the other, even if this may psychologically justify their reduction to the state of variables. It is a matter of strictly respecting the order of the dualities' formulation, MA or the inverse, and other inverted products since everything depends upon the order followed in knowledge and experience. Dualities are not indifferent and cannot be read in just any sense. It is impossible to determine both man and animal at the same time, an indeterminacy will follow. The MA product and vice versa does not make much sense unless their terms are reduced to the state of variables, which is justified in a project of rigorous understanding and not obviously in a naturalistic project. What do these variables mean? First their vectorialization or their apriority in an abstract Hilbert space normed by the imaginary number, not a Kantian apriority of space and time. A and M as biologically represented have nothing to do with this algebra. A science does not deal directly with phenomena, but just through the intermediary of symbols and the *a priori*, for example. The true "transcendental" condition is the matrix that conditions the *a priori* and makes possible their transformation into symbols, this is the function of the last-instance or the generic. It is not at all A which is the imaginary number and M idempotence in general, but it is M and A as variables which are both *a priori* subtracted by the square root of -1 within the matrix. But it is only (animalized) M who is duplicated and serves as an index for the *a priori*, through idempotence rather than the One of sufficiency.

The generic dimension is not the simple redoubling of man that the indexing by and to philosophy has proposed, it implies an indexing of variables and the whole matrix to superposition as a transcendental dimension of the Universe. Redoubling the scientific variable is not its multiplication by itself, but the multiplication of the fusion of the two by one of them, which is the quantum. The duplication of the "science" variable must not be metaphysical but scientific itself and its indexing must be done to superposition as a witness for all quantum thought.

What does this indexing of one of the variables to either philosophy or the quantum mean, how is it possible? It is a simple or unilateral duplication of the experience beyond the boundary of their fusion, there are not two lived experiences on the other side of the matrix but a single lived in two positions or halves, as if the scientific variable divided itself on either side of the matrix into a variable and an index, so that the generic may generate or retroactively assume the matrix as unilateral in relation to generic indexing. The generic or indexed scientific variable is extra-territorial and intra-territorial to the matrix in its nucleus of fusion. To put it in a succinct and abbreviated way, the complete matrix of the in-the-last-humanity is the idempotent conjugation of the imaginary number with itself. In particular, the 1 of the variable that is indexed to superposition is divided into two parts 1 and remains 1, this is idempotence. The variable that will play this double game is split into two functions, as an internal variable of the fusion matrix and as an index, these two 1s are linked in an analytically strong way (because of their duality and splitting) and synthetically weak (synthesis gains nothing and yet there is a synthesis). It is both a redoubling of the variable and a splitting of the variable that returns to the same, 2 fuses into 1 for the matrix and 1 divides into 2 for the generic. The generic is the One, always One but in two halves, not in the arithmetical sense of the Marxist dialectic, but within idempotence.

Man as "Algebraic Animal": Idempotence and Vector

How do we move from the matrix to the generic plane? In the description of the vectors that form the matrix it has already been said that they are the lived deducted from the philosophical or common subject and transformed under brand-new conditions of vectoriell configuration and lived materiality (Kant would say that this is formal intuition). As for the generic, it is reached as human last-instance if idempotence is its scientific or algebraic form. We suspect that between idempotence and lived vectoriality, as in Kant between concept and intuition (between the originally synthetic unity of apperception and formal intuition), there is a problem of schematism that the transcendental imagination provided Kant with a solution for. In our problematic it is necessary to rise once again from formal intuition to a generic condition, which is the idempotence of the lived or in-the-last-humanity.

A quantum matrix of fusion and superposition of variables, in order to become generic, is required to be reoriented by the duplication of one of its variables, life being then entirely under-determined either as vegetable, or as animal, or even as human. As generic in the strong sense, it is man who reorients it because he is virtually alone a generic being, capable of a duplication (or a splitting) called "idempotent", which is not arithmetic but algebraic. Idempotent, man is no longer separately animal or rational (with the subsequent mixtures). We will pass from the idempotence to the vector which are the two extreme poles of the construction by way of symmetry proper to transcendence. Transcendence transforms the real vector into an *objective vector* or splits it and redoubles it, and it is the place of schematism that is thus created, the function of the imagination lending itself to idempotence.

In other words, transcendence, transformed vectorially into an "objective" appearance, or into an objective vector by the real vector, must receive the intellectual and algebraic form of idempotence, which this time scientifically objectifies the imaginary appearance of the objective vector. We therefore distinguish between the apparent objectivity of the imagination and its strictly scientific objectification, which is the generic. The generic completes quantum objectification and moves it to Being-in-the-last-humanity. There is a general reorientation of the lived through the indexing to science. The vectoriell matrix is duplicated/split by the nature of idempotence, this is the generic or Being-in-the-last-humanity. This brings together the real vector, the rule of idempotence, and the imagination, on the basis of the objective vector that carries out their synthesis. This state, at once lived and idempotent of man, is now his only difference with the animal and the plant, his only addition to them and in a sense to himself as a specific anthropos. He under-determines the MAP system, therefore for man as well as for the animal or the plant. Because only man can possess this algebraic system, it is not an essence for all eternity but an operative process, a minimal logos, the minimum necessary calculation or possible language and not a sufficient or essential account. This double situation of man makes him related to MAP and at the same makes him into the Being-in-the-last-humanity that under-determines the three types of living things.

Finally, one should not confuse the modulated orientation as an elevation by idempotence, which simulates philosophy because of the lived experience that idempotence carries with it (without being such as the identity of understanding, which is largely a transcendent faculty), with the collapse as it is carried out by the real vector under-determining transcendence as a probable subject. The generic as algebraic is not in itself a fall because what collapses is the double transcendence rather than the algebraic rule. Obviously, the generic or effective idempotence, meaning "Being-in-the-last-humanity" beyond or below this simple rule, will be both a real subtraction and an ideal elevation. Moreover, it is not a reorientation through the duplication of "ordinary" or common man, but of the vector that is subjected to idempotence, and this orientation is produced as an overcoming toward generic man. But this one or the in-the-last-humanity is first vectoriell and lived, while being algebraic. This overall structure carries with it a lot of the lived but as what is no longer hierarchical and dominant; the generic human is not a philosophical man that is simply modified, but he is lowered into his very structure and by it.

5

THE UNIFICATION OF THE LIVED-WITHOUT-LIFE AND BEING-IN-THE-LAST-HUMANITY

Biological Unification and Generic Unification of the Living

Philosophy presupposes a unification of life as a maximum hierarchy in favor of Life as absolute over the living, as a minimal or asymptotic hierarchy through evolutionary or biological science. Bio-logico-philosophical unifications are based upon sufficient reason or sufficient life, and therefore upon transcendence, and proceed through over-determination of individuals by the living *a priori*, and then by the latter either through theology (a creation according to the divine plan of salvation) or through natural evolution. Darwin represents a first biological, unitary, and positive unification that could be interpreted as inclining the matrix toward the animal side, whereas we have reoriented or titled it toward the human side, but not theologically. Creationism and Darwinism are two opposing theories that must be suspended. The three major stages of unification are Aristotle, Descartes (the modern problem of the body and soul and then of mind), and Darwin. In the brute physics of the man-animal, MAP neighbor each other or are related (Darwin) and are in continuity, the continuum of life that feeds philosophy, and from this representation's point of view they form the chain of living things as properties or variables of life's flux. Each represents packets of communicating properties, exchanged and mixed with differences at first, sometimes of degrees and sometimes of nature. The Darwinian biologico-positive chain and its branches imposes the tendency to erase all difference of theological origin, but does not impose a reduction to the state of distinct variables within the limits of a matrix that would impose the formalization of these macroscopic packets as *a priori* productive forces or variables that can be conjugated. The continuism of most of these hypotheses, including the "differential," tolerates macroscopic differences (the pilot in his ship, the soul and the body), or asymptotic approximations such as animal culture, the animal's almost-symbolic, almost-language, almost-affectivity, and almost-technology, without inversely counting the decidedly or hopelessly animal character of M. Hence a whole culture of the encounter between man and animal through affectivity, language, and care. We are gradually entering into an animal culture, which is a postmodern way of responding to old problems of body and mind, causing them to abandon their speculative character for descriptions that are always right and validate prejudices

But we can also apply the principles of formal and vectoriell unification of theories exemplified by quantum physics to MAP relations, because there are in fact traditionally two/three possible theories or at least three *a priori* of the lived. The three modalities of the living can be treated effectively as the three *a priori* of life unified in the place of transcendent theories. MAP are the three *a priori* from which we draw and receive our relationship to life, which is to say to the lived. This is an extension and functional relaxation of the *a priori* which is no longer formal in the sense of rationalism, but vectoriell and materiell. The layer of the *a priori* is important within the transcendental quantum, but here it is not a question of some objectification of life in line with the model of the hard sciences' transcendental objectification.

Generic unifications are based upon constraints that ensure the discreetness of the real and so upon a subtraction and under-determination. Regarding continuist theories, priority will be given the discreetness of the quantum of the lived, which imposes limits on philosophical interpretations of life (for Bohr, discreetness is what limits classical physics and its concepts), and highlights the vectoriality of life as projected. The quantum of the lived (not exactly of humanity) is the nonquantum equivalent of energy or action, it is the threshold from which life begins for the living (even for the plant). Against the impression of the vague character of the lived as indeterminate and unarticulated energy, it must be stated that the lived is not continuous but discreet. This discreetness is not spatial as Bergson thinks it is and in returning to discreetness, we move away from his position in particular. The lived constant is discreet so that it can be treated scientifically and in a microscopic way and not in a macroscopic way as a continuum. Energy is discreet, so why shouldn't the lived that replaces it be? It is important not to confuse the lived with consciousness and the flux of macroscopic consciousness, the difference is less about substantial representation than method and access to the real. And even if we confuse the flux and the particle as quantum thought allows, it is still no longer the flow of consciousness but the discreet lived. There will be knowledge about life that is not the consciousness of life. Neither Darwin and his naturalism nor Bergson and his spiritualism (these being philosophical positions drawn from biology or spirituality) respond to a specific or lived constant which is neither naturalistic or materialist, nor spiritualist, meaning not ultimately based upon consideration of the living.

In the description of vectors it has already been said that they are the lived withdrawn from the philosophical or common subject and transformed under totally new conditions of abstraction and materiality. The substance of the generic constant as human is ultimately the idempotent lived and idempotence is its scientific or algebraic form. The materiell lived that comes from physics and psychology passes to the generic state when, not related to itself within the reflection of a living thing, it is indexed upon idempotence. The constant of the lived guarantees a scientific position (meaning a human and not theological or creationist one) to the problem of life.

Anthropological Cut and Generic Cut: The Non-Separability of the Lived

We have generally questioned eco-logical difference as it is part of the anthropo-logic cut that defines man as a "rational animal" facing the natural environment, man as a synthesis of the animal subject and the attribute "rational," or some other attribute. It is an ambiguous cut by way of a reciprocal encroachment of the subject and the attribute, or a reversible one, the two determining each other reciprocally in a superior mixture so that man is a "logical animal." The Aristotelian formula seems, however, like the quantum, to render the animal-subject non-commutative with the logos as a human property, but this is a false noncommutativity. In reality it ends in reversibility or a superior unity of a metaphysical symmetry. This cut is the basis of an ecology whose norms are philosophical because difference is never sufficiently subtractive or under-determining in relation to philosophical over-determination. The classical subject-attribute, animal-rational structure can well be replaced by that of the *Dasein*-world structure, by that of ontologico-ontic difference, or with other structures, it is always a variation on the same structure of difference.

As for the generic cut, it is first defined as quantum and not as anthropo-logical. We apply what is called the "quantum formalization" of Heisenberg (ap . . . pa)hi, which combines the inverted products with h (Planck's constant) and i (the imaginary number), and we stop using metaphysics' causal determinism between animal, reason, and man. We no longer see being-human (rational) and being-animal (biological) as macroscopic instances but as two simple properties or variables of the lived. We must "split" man, who is no longer the synthesis of animal and rationality, but a system that supports a double quantum state. The "logos" is no longer the main attribute for the subject "animal," but a property next to animality. The quantum requires that we "split" the human subject as a generic subject into his two properties or states, as animal (or animal within man) and as rational (within the animal). Generic man is at least in two states but is not confused with their synthesis or their analysis.

The ecological understanding of life is a series of theoretical operations that finally combine major structures, the generic order completing and giving its meaning to the matrix or vectoriell construction that serves as its base or its infrastructure. Here is a quick schema. For these two orders to combine they need to execute all the phases of understanding (preparation of superposition, quantification properly speaking, random experimentation, indexing) concerning the material of the three MAP givens which are the base data or which serve as variables in the matrix. These three givens are considered as formal *a priori* for the intuition of life and then serve, by way of inversion of function, as formal intuition (see Kant) or a constitutive vectoriell for life, and finally they are unified through an indexing to the superposition within the generic of the in-the-last-humanity. The order of construction goes from the experience of life to life in its understanding in-the-last-humanity through the vectoriell architecture of the three *a priori*, and then through being indexed to the dimension of the universe. This assumes that these three givens are quantumly and generically under-determined by the concreteness of the generic matrix that sets its functional status in each of the phases of the matrix.

Quantum (and generic) cuts are therefore organized around the conjugable but non-commutative variables of animalized rational man and the humanized animal, but only if their non-separability is established. This non-separability of man and the animal within man and outside of man, the refusal to separate them as macroscopic entities, can be stated in four senses. Obviously, these four distinct statuses imply a certain separability that must be evaluated. These forms are the following: 1. man-animal as generic-in-the-last-humanity, this is our object-of-knowledge; 2. man-animal as in itself and the philosophical mixture of the subject and the predicate of reason, this is our real-object or material drawn from philosophy; 3. man-animal as humanized or culturalized clone drawn especially from the philosophical subject when it is under-determined as generic; 4. man-animal as "animalized" clone drawn particularly from the animal, this man animalized or for various reasons lowered to his anti-human low-water mark. This complex subject will therefore be said in three/four senses since there will be the mediate between the two extreme meanings. We need two clones, the humanized or culturalized animal and animalized man.

Let us repeat this with reference to separability: 1. the macroscopic man-animal composed of two entities, sometimes separable and sometimes not, with a not quite relative blending or non-separability, this is the given philosophical material; 2. man-animal as non-separable or entangled, but separated as a "generic man" defined or known himself in a probable way; 3. as a clone. Being identical to the function of-the-last-instance, generic man under-determines the clone, and therefore the animal-man and their relative separability, this is the "humane" under-determination of the animal-man.

The Non-Separability of Man and Animal as Variables and their Separability In-the-Last-Instance

Let us suppose that M and A are not inseparable under a transcendent and ultimately religious unity, both angels and beasts, but inseparable and not localizable for quantum reasons. Humans and animals are no longer a macroscopic question of localizable entities identified in a concept, their problem presents itself at a more complex level of thought, not in a biologico-philosophical framework but at least in the context of a quantum formalism if not a structural one. It is indeed necessary to distinguish two similar kinds of solutions, a rather Marxist solution of the structural fusion of opposites, and another of non-commutative quantum variables in superposition instead.

If it is a simple fusion (M/A), as in Marx's structuralism for example, which is not yet a "true" superposition, the question arises in any case about going further than a choice between this fusion but under the animal thus redoubled (the human is achieved and complete if he also remains an animal), and this fusion under humanity thus redoubled (the animal is complete and achieved if it is also humanized). Animals are only animals, but shaped by human culture. Humans are only humans, but shaped by animality. This is the only way to solve the problem of their common unity and their unilateral difference if we give ourselves a form of non-separability that tolerates an ultimate distinction.

The M/A non-separability, if it must surpass this structural conception, is not that of two instances reunited under a transcendent unity, with exchanges and mixtures, but an immanent unity that is this time a superposition of vectors distinguished as the addition of a mixed analysis or synthesis. M and A cease to be treated as transcendent or biological species, as macroscopic bodies reduced to resemblances regarding their respective understanding, and should instead be treated as variables or properties of the subject = X, which will in any case be M/A. Obviously, the formula of non-separability is negatively stated, but it is positive if it is also the irreducible minimum for breaking or for blending, a quantum of life that tolerates a difference, more precisely a quantum of the lived that is suitable only for man in what will be his function as last-instance.

From the Quantum of the Lived to the In-the-Last-Humanity (1)

The imaginary number is necessary to make a matrix of vectors out of man/animal, it is enough to have the philosophical givens concerning man and concerning the animal, to merge them through the matrix. The quantum is not an identity but a measure or a relation, it is a scientific concept of invariance, necessary to think human phenomena as holistic or non-separable, also random, an extension of quantum holism that is not the whole but non-separability extended to the limits of philosophy. If the human quantum is based upon animal-man non-separability (or reason), then it is not enough.

Non-separability has several interpretations, at least three. The quantum here is not quantitative, nor philosophical or analytical/synthetic, but it is at least an invariance that can be the cogito's equivalent. It is necessary to try non-separability in a minimal philosophical way, to show that this solution is limited, that it is able to be conceived by the matrix and imaginary number instead. Non-separability signifies that a quasi "synthesis" is carried out by an instance of the One, whatever its form, for example through a superposition, and that there is at least one continuity between (rational) man and animal even if the two do not play the same role, as this unity precisely excludes simple sameness. Is it an identity through a transcendental-and-immanent One, so therefore a classical transcendental One? The One or non-separability is first of all a holism-All according to a vague philosophical definition, but its necessarily quantum and generic treatment changes everything. The quantum of humanity is not a number but the generic or complete matrix, it is a quantification adapted to the definition of humanity.

However, the quantum is not the continuous One, it is a decisive factor of the (idempotent) constant of a human algebra and not of a humanist philosophy provided that it is understood simply as the One of the non-separability animal-man or man-nature which is, for example, at the basis of Marx's formula, and which, as a developed matrix, says that man is a natural being (non-separable, man-animal fusion) who makes nature human (nature therefore indexed to man). However, quantum non-separability as entanglement is not really thought by Marx, who speaks about them all as separated metaphysical entities, or without the quantum, and projects all of it into a philosophical matrix. Marx states this non-separability in the style of torsion, man is an animal (for example, or a sentient being, this is non-separability or one of its interpretations), but makes the animal human (this is the true ecological aim). We need a matrix of contraries as non-separables in an immanent way or as relative separability, but where everything happens "under the human," which is not idealist because man is here identical to science and not ultimately understood "under the animal." The animal is *physis*, but physical science is on the side of man and not of nature or in any case touches nature only by way of man. Marx remains materialist without submitting everything to the animal, undoubtedly, but because he remains within a classical physics.

From the Quantum of the Lived to the In-the-Last-Humanity (2)

We are looking to determine generic man, not only as a real object but now as an under-determined object of knowledge without deterministic causality. We are not talking about the last man or the end of humanity, that kind of utopia is not ours, but about humanity of-the-last-instance or the in-the-last-humanity. We are trying to think under this ultimate condition, which prohibits their confusion or their overlap, the MAP non-separability in a way that is neither naturalist or theological, neither creationist or Darwinian, this latter point of view is not sufficient, even if it is much better than the opposite one. We are blurring philosophy's dualities and traditional identifications, which no longer seems to us to be able to do justice to man, to the animal, and to plants.

There is a threshold of humanity, a "Planck's humanity," below which we cannot descend because its lower limit is set by what we call generic indexing. It is not some metaphysical human nature, but is at least a human nature such that physics can contribute to its determination within certain limits. The quantum of humanity is not a number but the generic matrix, it is a matrix and generic quantification for the definition of humanity. The subject = X is what we call generic man or what defines or determines in-the-last-humanity the MAP system in its entirety, including man. What we call "generic man" is thus derived from the animal, the plant, and specifically humans in the narrowest sense, which passes through three states, there is a triplicity of states to be prepared. MAP are no longer species separated according to a biological distribution, but point to another theory, that of states of the lived.

The first fundamental gesture is to say that if MAP are properties treated as variables, then the subject = X will distinguish itself from their possible states. But the second gesture is to say that the generic cut now indexes (with a retroactive effect) these variables as properties of the generic subject = X, measured or calibrated by it as a "transcendental" dimension of the superposition that also belongs to the matrix. This means treating them generically in a second gesture, not only as lived vectors forming an infrastructure but as a generic or quasi-subjective superstructure. As a result, generic man will have an identity in the form of a quantum superposition, meaning in a "Universe" dimension and not a "World" one.

There is a quantum of humanity that enriches the quantum of the lived properly so-called, which is valid for the human sciences and which is not the circle of transcendent unity and reversibility of the animal with the predicate of the logos. At the very least the quantum apparatus, and so the imaginary number, are required. A human quantum assumes MAP non-separability as a basis, predicates that finally form a circle within philosophy against all appearance (that which ratiocinate ecology tries to overcome) and from there are indexed viciously by it to man instead of being generically and by the matrix indexed to the superposition so that man(-animal) and the animal(-man) definitively abandon their commutativity in the turns and detours of a superhumanism or transhumanism.

The question of the quantum as an externally fixed natural constant is not yet that of its immanent understanding. The quantum of ("ordinary") humanity is therefore not an understanding obtained externally and positively, but generic man can determine this quantum himself in a non-vicious circle, despite its being obtained through traditional philosophical knowledge, though capable of knowing himself or under-determining himself without auto-determination. We therefore distinguish the human (on the way to being generic) as a MAP fusion that is the quantum of the lived properly speaking, and also its indexing as a generic human indexed to superposition as a form of the Universe. That is to say, an inseparable triplicity of lived experiences, and their indexation understood as "generic-oriented." The quantum would be the physically modeled treatment of non-separability and the generic would be the indexing to man as a subject of quantum knowledge, that is, of the Universe. The in-the-last-humanity associates with and fuses the matrix as the natural process of the probable subject, and with superposition as the form of objective knowledge to which it is indexed.

We take as our point of view the three living things and not life's generality. In order to treat the problems of MAP according to their ecological environment in particular, we have been considering them all as living beings. But they are not modes of physical matter or the psyche, even if they have some of these properties, they are properties or variables of life's flux. The living are defined as a matrix by two variables much like a chessboard square and not by a metaphysical essence, be it natural or theological. This is a way of restoring some sense, but through the matrix, to the unity of body and mind and to respond to this problem in a different way, by dealing with packets or (non-commutative) dualities of state vectors giving shape to the properties of the living.

It was therefore necessary to have a constant specific to this lived environment of life. However, this constant, which we specify totally as anthropic, is the lived said to be "of-the-last-humanity." The quantum of the lived as a constant has its equivalent or generic respondent in the humanity of-the-last-instance. The lived-without-life is the constant of a new matter, specific and irreducible for both physics and psychology. Life as lived in-the-last-humanity is a phenomenological domain that refuses physical, psychological reduction, even simple biological reduction, and merges instead with the generic. The generic converts the under-determination of MAP, of their product or their matrix, into a human mode.

In some way we have given two definitions of the quantum of life. What is the relationship between the quantum of the lived and man's before-priority? There is nothing that can serve as the quantitative measure for the quantum of the lived that is formal. What distinguishes a generic science from a positive science as well as from a philosophy? The constant of the lived is not objective like the physical constants are, but must be "reprised" or "converted" as generic and made consistent through idempotence and not through a reflexive identity. This is what distinguishes a generic science (not exactly a "human" one) from a purely positive science, there is a conversion of the constant of the lived by placing it under idempotence rather than classically under identity. Why a "reprise"? Let us compare the in-the-last-humanity or "generic human reality" with Heidegger's *Dasein*. The difference is between the *Ur-transcendenz* of *Dasein* and vectoriell ascending, between the still theological existentiality of ontological difference and algebraic vectoriality. What is at stake is the human experience of life or of the in-the-last-lived in the general sense of life, it under-determines all of the living things. What is therefore presented is the problem of a threshold of generic humanity for life, not only of a quantum of the lived but of humanity, a kind of "Planck's humanity" undoubtedly, but which is at the same time capable of knowing itself, thought without going through a reflection. It involves indexing the lived to the Universe or superposition, this is the distinctive feature of man who knows himself without being a "self-"reflection. *Any transcendent and naturalistic essence must be substituted, not by the theory of life, but with the understanding of life by itself.* It is a question of going back not to man, which is theology, but to life or to the generic living thing to which the understanding indexed to the Universe gives meaning. And even to the living thing endowed with knowledge of itself without being for that quasi-reflexive as is *Dasein* indexed to the World through its transcendence. The generic human settles their problems through idempotence and not through ontological difference. Man is redoubled in his act of knowledge added generically, man is self-knowledge as generic and not as metaphysical. If there is no longer only a quantum of the lived that is quasi-physical, but instead a true Planck's humanity indexed this time to the quantum and so to the Universe, it will be physical but enveloped in the thought (of) itself understood as the idempotence of theory and its object and no longer as an analytical or synthetic identity, or even a reflexive one. What does this formula of life's knowledge (of) itself mean? That it will not immediately be given as superior for theological reasons, because the anthropic distinction is that of knowledge and not that of anthropo-logy limited to Being-in-the-world. Anthropo-logy is therefore replaced by the physics of man as the last-humanity knowing its situation within the World and outside of the World. We substitute the quantum of life, below which we cannot go any further, for that essence or for that human nature assumed to be impassable and enclosing a threshold limit. The constant of the lived is the lowest or minimum limit that cannot be exceeded, it signals the discreetness of human life and so of all life. The quantum possesses a divided depth or duality. A double limit in reality, an upper limit that lowers philosophical pretensions concerning life, and a lower limit that stops its materialist and physicalist reduction. This lower and upper limit is set by what is no longer "human nature," except as the model of physics can (co-)determine and as it relates to itself by idempotence. How is this a threshold below which we cannot go past without risking losing the knowledge of life? It is so in that the living human being is always obliged to assume it in all circumstances as a "last-instance" but indexed to themselves (idempotence) or generically.

From Being-in-the-world to Being-for-the-universe

How can the human sciences be re-built upon a new division and a new non-philosophical experience of man? Generic man is the new quantum, the measure or more exactly the minimum of discreet humanity. Philosophy forms an excessive and overly broad correlation at the extremes with the singular subject and God. The idea that humanity is a historically continuous flux between the animals and God, between the infra-human and the overhuman, is for example the Nietzschean foundation of the human sciences. This philosophical continuum is at the root of superhumanism and technological transhumanism as it goes back and forth on this rope, this bridge stretched over the abyss. The other error responds to this continuum, the individual dispersion, the other historical conception of the chain of being, albeit more modern than theological. For this ascending chain of life we substitute the quanta of humanity or the lived, which replaces the division of humanity into races, diverse properties, families, biological divisions, etc. It is obviously possible to divide it according to the sciences or the aspects we take human beings to be under. However, it is a matter here of a science of man by man in the sense sought by Hobbes, Hume, and Rousseau, and so this is not history, sociology, or the human sciences, but an immanent (able to be quantumly modeled) science of the lived human of the last-instance and more broadly of the lived (experiences) of other "kingdoms." Generic science is not a science of nature, but at best of human nature, quantum modeling this science of humans. These are not causes of the classical kind or have not been lived with any efficiency, formality, materiality, or metaphysical purpose but are of another nature, they are the determination-in-the-last-instance of before-priority (by superposition) of these transcendent forms of causality.

This generic quantum is not defined as something given by another science, by philosophy and theology as a creature or as a living biological body, but defined by generic science itself which sets the quantum within certain modalities. The generic constant is very different from the ones found in physics and even in phenomenology, which present themselves as absolutes, because the generic constant is obtained within an immanent process of knowledge and therefore remains random or uncertain. A characteristic constant of an object is not a subject, but here the constant is applicable to the variables where there is the subject, a science, and philosophy especially. Philosophy itself has no rigorous human quantum, it is replaced by the soul, mind, body, transcendence, etc. In this context we need one which breaks with the metaphysical continuity and absolute discontinuity of the subject copied from the modern multiple, as the errant subject is.

The Amplitude of the "Christ" Symbol Lowered as Generic Man and Mediator of the Universe

Let us assume for now that quantum theory and philosophy are the best frameworks for our problem, before we see if we can integrate other kinds of knowledge here. It is important to make philosophy a knowledge like any other but as basic, which suddenly cancels out the excessive difference between apparently modest generic procedures and philosophical sufficiency. The objective of generic science is to reduce philosophy through the quantum and thus to liberate other knowledges or to rewrite them otherwise with philosophy. It is inevitable that we will be given to reference those disciplines of knowledge that are more transmittable than the others, more critical also of themselves and other activities. They do not produce truths in themselves, eternal, a scale of essences with the papacy represented by philosophy. Generic science is not the expression of a narrowly physicist or physicalist ideal, it conjugates the quantum and philosophy as quantum variables themselves (hence the procedure of indexing and not only of vectorialization). So that their connection has a strong or double relation to humans as subjects of knowledges, together they form determination in-the-last-instance and can therefore be invested in the theory of art, love, politics, and religion. It is impossible to reconstruct a theological or aristocratic scale of truths that would form a heavenly paradise in the name of philosophy. Impossible to accept this architecture that has so little of the human and democratic about it; determination-in-the-last-instance prohibits it.

The quantum matrix and its superposition as an imaginary number fulfills the role of a human basis since everything about man is then derived from quantum physics and from its quasi-reflexivity through indexing. If there is a procedure to reach the subject, it is knowledge itself as generic. Generic man is defined as a system = X or a human state through complex lived vectors, and we distinguish the knowledge that we have of him like we distinguish a constant and the transcendental way of producing or knowing it.

The theory of the generic matrix, both quantum and generic, should allow a reprise of the anthropic principle's meaning, which would lower it in its sufficiency and reformulate it as last-instance that under-determines the vectorialization of states and does so in a circle that is no longer altogether vicious. The classical physical formulation of the anthropic principle has something obvious and vicious about it, but if it is understood as last-instance then generic man is indeed the lived heart of the Universe and his belonging to it is what makes it possible to think about the Universe. What we call generic humanity of-the-last-instance is such that, as indexed to the Universe, it uses the quantum and therefore its object, the Universe, to know itself. Generic man is made up of vectors, he is locally modifiable but he must become invariant for all and despite all these local modifications. This invariance can only be obtained by relating state vectors (with their variable phases) to themselves, meaning to the imaginary number. Under the condition of the complex number, the state vector thus acquires the ontological power of the under-determination of the particles of the Universe and of humanity itself. We move from the generic man prepared in the matrix to the man of the last-instance knowing himself as under-determined. The Universe is the correlate of humanity of-the-last-instance, which should make possible a critique of the principle of anthropic sufficiency that, in the current physicist form, is a simple philosophical vicious circle. We have found and oppose to it a *principle of anthropic non-sufficiency*.

The principles of the unification of theories exemplified by physics are applied here to MA relations. Traditionally there are two theories for the living with a basis in philosophical unification (M as animalized logos, A as weakly humanized or without-logos). As we have said, the three major stages of unification are Aristotle, Descartes (the modern problem of the body and the soul and then the mind), and Darwin. Darwin represents a biological unification or a leaning toward the animal side. Creationism and Darwinism are two opposing theories of unification. It is therefore the principle or means of these kinds of logico- or bio-philosophical unifications that must be challenged because they are based upon sufficient reason and more generally upon the principle of sufficient anthropo-logy or upon the principle of anthropological sufficiency. Either upon theology or upon natural evolution, either creation according to the divine plan of salvation, or upon the history of life ending in man. They tolerate mixtures, macroscopic distances (the pilot in his ship) and also a certain number of local experimental verifications such as animal culture, the almost-symbolic, the almost-language, almost-affectivity, and almost-technology of the animal without countering the decidedly or desperately animal character of man. These mixtures are symptoms of the non-separability of MA and should no longer be interpreted as mixtures between two macroscopic poles but as simple matrix variables or properties of a non-separable entity $= X$, which is the true subject of the matter. It is therefore necessary to find a new form of objectification of (for) these mixtures and no longer one transferred from them and repeating them within theory.

This is the great generic unification of life by the lived against theology (or intelligent design) but also against Darwin's biological naturalism, which cannot explain the before-priority of generic man. Hence the following central hypothesis of this essay. Creationism will be avoided, as will naturalism, through recourse to this point of theoretical unification: Christ as symbol of generic man before-first or as the in-the-last-humanity, as a point of transmutation meaning superposition of the biological-naturalist interpretations of Darwin and

Christian theologico-naturalist ones, which are both lowered by the generic man = X who supports them. This solution seems to be so paradoxical and so apparently unscientific, that for us it is still Christ who is the theoretical pivot (obviously not historical or religious) of the generic and who introduces it into history or into the World, or more precisely makes it come out within-the-last-humanity, that is to say, to be even more precise, makes it enter the Universe as a correlate of the in-the-last-humanity. The whole problem is one of changing the frame of reference, there are at least two frames and not just one like philosophy believes, it is uniform but otherwise than for philosophy, for all observers. Christ is just the symbol of what each human now is as an individual observer of the Universe. This thesis is not Copernican, it is not part of the history of astronomy, not even of astrology . . . but of physics which has made the Universe an object of science. What we call Christ has nothing to do with first or empirical ecology, except for a few biblical logia, it goes without saying that the humanized animal and animalized man are no more commutative than Christ is with the World. Christ extends humanity to the dimensions of the Universe, this is a new amplitude that is offered to humans, not only an amplitude of technique but of thought and of life. He takes away the death of the World by bringing forth resurrection into the Universe.

Quantum Collapse as Degrowth of Philosophical Man

Philosophy's degrowth is at the same time the degrowth of the image of man given by philosophy. There is no point in simply opposing man and philosophy, which risks returning to a gnosis impregnated by religion without modifying both in a spirit that is both physical and generic. But it is urgent that a new place for man is found in relation to an ecological science of life.

The maxim of a quantum physicist is decisive for us, at least as a symptom of the cost of a "blank" that makes it difficult to understand: "Nature preceded man, but man preceded the sciences of Nature" (von Weizsäcker cited by Heisenberg). If we take this formula literally, we will have only replaced philosophy's privilege with that of science for man, so that the only difference would be that of two disciplines. A new, more fundamental formulation of this chiasmus is here assumed in order to restore the right relations of before-priority, priority, and equality, which structures the edifice of life and that have been simplified and flattened by philosophy in the work of our physicist author. Nature, as animal, precedes man or prevails over him in priority and inversely, but the science that man can be is as-before-priority over priority itself and so over the man-animal. In other words, all science suffers from philosophy and its influence, but a so-called generic science does not suffer it without also carrying it along with it in its baggage and reducing its priority to the state of a simple variable. This is not only a more malleable formulation than philosophy, it reveals the repressed truth that guarantees it as a symptom. It is the same substitution of order for hierarchy, or even of an order that includes philosophical hierarchy as one of its variables for its quantum use. We grant only a mitigated belief to those who, driven by their observant and animal passion, affirm that the animal not only knows but knows that it knows, confusing the ruses of strategy with the Idea of the Idea, invention and learning linked to need with the most abstract knowledge, calculation with mathematics, and habits of the den with knowledge of the cosmos.

It is still necessary to have serious reasons, last and perhaps eschatological reasons, to further distinguish humans from the rest of creation, not by way of a supplement of dominant properties of the same nature but on the contrary by a power of subtraction (of) itself or a reserve that forms its true non-animal and non-vegetative force. What we steal from the algebraists to give to human beings—generic idempotence—is more a state of weakness than of force, a state of weak force or a collapse, a caving in, at the very least a lowering-over rather than a supplement of force. Man is not an empire within an empire, but precisely because he alone can renounce it in constituting himself always and spontaneously as an animal or plant empire. This new order is not a hierarchy within a common element or a univocal generality. Priority and hierarchy go together in philosophy as first, while before-priority or last-humanity imposes the equality of man, animal, and plant, but adds the power to man, not only to bring the whole of nature under a science like the rest of nature, but of being able to operate or to be a performatively scientific animal, and in particular a mathematician in the broadest sense of the term. The idempotent addition of this possibility to human animality is quite different from that of the rational attribute to Aristotle's individual subject or, for example, from the Nietzschean will to power to the forces that make up the fabric of life. For it is not in Nietzsche's or Aristotle's case an idempotent and algebraic addition that would impose an order without hierarchy, but that of a supplement of transcendence in the immanence of forces and which ends, as we know, with an eminently Greek and metaphysical apology for the overman and not with the equality of the natural orders of life released by subtraction. Democracy is possible within a rigorous use of philosophy, but it is impossible in philosophy's use of itself when it auto-models itself.

The hypothesis we are forming is different than that of the philosophers, who set their ideal in over-humanity, rejecting the old desire for domination and the hubris of super-humanization. On the quantum side, which is not the only one that has to come under consideration, this hypothesis is that of a falling into or a collapse of this humanity, of a degrowth of man's metaphysical nature as a living thing and therefore of his hegemonic function within nature that reveals itself as an appearance or an irreality. And on the generic side, which completes the quantum as associated and is under-determined by it, that correlative degrowth of its function as a sufficient subject rooted in the metaphysical sky is corrected by the reconstitution of a certain subjectivity, but generically and not as a substitution. It is also comes from the subtractive despite its nature as a rule, meaning as a before-first reference or, depending on the meaning of the chosen causality, as a last-humanity. Since both quantum and generic modelings of life are intimately linked, their overall effect is that of a general subtractive state of ruin for all the possible eco-logical relationships. They are entirely composed of algebraic functions that alleviate the edifice of macroscopic ecology and the MAP system of any substantial determination.

A quantum collapse of philosophical humanity or a falling into its ruins, its generic reduction, its knowledge marked by probability, humanity changing places within nature and the world, repositioned at the center of the universe but at the point of its knowledge alone, all of this produces a cloud of misunderstandings that assails us here. Knowledge of life and man in particular, even of the in-the-last-humanity, is affected by indeterminacy or uncertainty with regard to its philosophical representation, and generically through a lack of sufficient identity or reflection. "In relation to its philosophical representation" means that the essence of quantumly objectified generic humanity is not a supplement of force or will, the movement by leap or by continuity to a superhuman being, but rather a collapse of that humanity, that is to say, of the old man and his sufficiency drawn from the World as the source of all sufficiency. A collapse that is not an intra-historical and contingent event but a positive structure specific, as we have already said elsewhere, to the "weak force of victims" and to the generic knowledge that they have of themselves. To speak of a decline of philosophical humanity is not to be a "declinist," a falling down or collapse is not an apocalypse, degrowth is not a flight into the desert, and it may be all of this as well but in the now renewed transcendental sense tolerated by Reason-in-person. We must not deny or even deconstruct all of philosophy's terms, almost the whole of everyday language, but they must be reoriented according to the meaning of the causality chosen as the key to interpretation.

Subtraction and Lowered-over Transcendence

The imaginary number must be understood as a subtraction whose means are addition, without for that turning like a Möbius stripe and coming back into itself. It is not subtraction through the set-theoretical void but through the vector, a subtractive addition or a subtraction by addition. This is a way of solving the problem of the *infra/super*-structure cut such that immanence is from below (the surface or the horizon) by way of its origin, but functions as an addition or a transcendence which is therefore lowered, a simple ascending. The imaginary number is not the tip of absolute transcendence or an excess over itself like the tip of the Platonic Good or the Cartesian Cogito, its excessive essence is explained by its subtractive or negative being through the square root of -1, and not by a simple cumulative addition of whole and real unities. This is not a theological breach (Levinas, Derrida, Marion) but a positive state to be introduced into philosophy through quantum conjugation.

The difference is clear between 1. the double transcendence of classical philosophy which penetrates superficially into the ground like the root of a tree in order to rise up circularly and resurface *from below* (the root twice splits transcendence between the root, the trunk, and the branches), 2. Jewish transcendence, which is immediately absolute, not even double or theological, which starts from the self where it takes a positive foothold by affecting it without really taking root in it, an infinite transcendence absorbing rootedness in an absolute affect of the infinite, and finally 3. the imaginary number that starts *as-below or from-below* the waterline (which separates the wave-particle from the corpuscle) in order to ascend *but as immanence* and always from below but not *through the below*, as if it came first from somewhere else and continued into the going forth or in the ascent. This is the difference between scientific radicality and philosophical circularity, which are symmetrical but the first is "radical" and the second is "absolute." Scientific radicality does not return to the real that it has only apparently left, it is not a split macroscopic transcending but a single ascending without mixture or a circle of the two opposite directions (Husserl, for example). We thus distinguish the vectoriell infrastructure that contains the particle, and the objective and double super-structure that targets or contains the corpuscle.

We know from the quantum that there is a tunnel effect problem in articulating these two components (*infra/super*-structure) in a non-specular way. Where exactly is this tunnel? The difficulty comes the fact that two understandings are possible, either through the scientific way that starts from the particle in order to understand the corpuscle as decoherent, or through the inverse philosophical way, the "prepared" corpuscle allowing the particle to be understand as coherent. These ways are obviously scientifically complementary rather than simply reversed.

Assume a vector (coming from below or from the macroscopic and coherent region) targeting a corpuscle (this is decoherence) and returning toward another particle (this is coherence). On the way there it acts, coming anyway from below as an ascending, as a breakthrough or a "trans(breakthrough)" of the waterline or border that separates the two regions, *infra-* and *super*-structure. The ascending penetrates into the double transcendence or into the open air of the macroscopic or objective world, it becomes transcendence carried away or driven by the corpuscle's circle. On the way there, it is always a vectoriell ascending that acts. But when it returns, like a root, it is pierced from below in order to cross this border. The tunnel is at the return of the vector that comes from the corpuscle, or decoherence, it is the vector that pulls below the corpuscle and makes it immanent or coherent as a wave and particle, it lowers-over its transcendence or its decoherent state. The outward journey is the continuity of the vector and the trans-, there is no tunnel on the outward journey of the vector that hooks onto the corpuscle on its way and circulates with it. On this return it separates from the trans- and leaves it behind in the form of a circle of objective appearance. This is the solution to the problem of the infrastructure's articulation determinate for the super-structure and to the surface tunnel that moves backwards onto itself and onto its dotted path of the ascent. The movement from the microscopic or wave to the macroscopic corpuscle is unintelligible or dotted, but this unintelligibility is limited and relative to the world of the corpuscle, it is explained by the effect of circumstances exterior to the particle. On the other hand, the return of the vector from the corpuscle to the particle is intelligible as a process of knowledge that assumes a given exterior to the vector, a "preparation" and so a causality, but not a determinist one.

The Fourfold of Constants Constituting "Being-in-the-Last-Humanity"

Our point of view is not to establish a new ontic theory of life, something we are incapable of, but a theory concerning the knowledge of life. This perspective therefore has something of the transcendental about it, without for all that fulfilling the philosophical and Kantian concept of it. In any case, the two planes will not be cynically confused. Knowledge of life is itself a scientific object and like any scientific object it is structured according to constants which form a fourfold and that must be fixed first in order to frame and limit its process. A generic science of life is a duality of entangled structures: 1. on the one hand, the quantum model applied to the living things who host life implies its interpretation as lived and vectoriell materiality, forming materiells *a priori* for life as it is given-as-represented, this is the properly quantum aspect of this theory, 2. on the other hand, a generic reorientation of science that corrects its positivity offered too easily to philosophy, and conditions it in such a way that it will be called immanental instead of transcendental, while substituting itself for the One of philosophical sufficiency that runs through the great evolutionist interpretations of what have been discussed.

These two structures, which are like the infrastructure and superstructure, contain four constants. The constants of a so-called generic science of life are of multiple types, but crossed within a matrix and cannot have the simplicity they have within a positive science. They are formal and algebraic through the imaginary number implying the vectoriality of the real and the idempotence that substitutes itself for the One of sufficiency, thus ensuring the quantum matrix's generic character. But they are also material through the quantum postulate of the discreet lived or quantum of the lived, and through the three types of living things (MAP) which are material, quasi-physical, and biological constants. Two that are formal with a mathematical essence, two that are material and typical of life and biology.

1   Heisenberg's "quantum postulate" can be extended to life and not only in its molecular form as the code of life. Molecular biology only understands amino acids and requires a quantum leap at the level of chemistry. In any case, the quantum postulate is also decisive in the transcendental knowledge of life and not only for its chemistry, it is constitutive and not only a regulator of the discreet and indivisible lived. This is the material constant that is at the basis of a quantum of life (which will be extended into a constant of humanity that is formal and material at once). The quantum matrix therefore assumes the quantum of the lived replacing physical matter, this is the equivalent of the quantum of action or energy and is therefore something lived in the broad sense. The lived is the substance of life, its starting point and what limits any physical, psychological, or philosophical hold on it.

2   A second material but contingent constant, that of the three kinds of living things (the contingent MAP system) that express the lived. But this material constant can be understood at several levels, as an empirical and contingent given, and within the matrix as constituting three *a priori* or three relatively universal and necessary variables, which make it possible to objectify the lived.

3   A constitutive constant, both formal and intuitive, vectoriality, thus the imaginary number, inscribed in a Hilbert configuration space. A constant that is both geometric and algebraic and helps to define the real object that is the lived and to distinguish it from any representation.

4   Another formal constant specific to the generic dimensions, idempotence as an algebraic property that maintains close relations with the imaginary number and vectoriality through the philosophical variable. The materiell lived, taken from the physical and psychological lived but carried by philosophy, is first treated in a quantum way within the matrix, but it passes to the generic state when, not related to itself by human reflection in the manner of a philosophical subject, it is indexed to the algebraic factor of superposition and idempotence. From this point of view, we can carefully distinguish between Kantianism (originary synthetic unity of apperception = I think) and the algebraic solution of idempotence that will succeed it here as a generic factor.

Together they form the generic constant of the in-the-last-humanity. We will not confuse the content of the matrix with the scientific constant of the lived that is valid for the MAP system and the generic in so far as we understood it here in a non-commutative way. What raises philosophical sufficiency and its scientific modalities directly concerns man alone and is transmitted from man to the animal and to the plant but only in-the-last-instance. Man in the narrow sense, what we still call it, has ambiguous relationships of identity and communication with the animal and the plant. So that we will also distinguish man in the metaphysical and/or animal sense within the MAP system and his Being-in-the-last-humanity.

ECOLOGY AS QUANTUM OF THE MESSIANIC LIVED

Its Matrix Phases

There are three given kinds of living things or three contingent stases of life, equal or without hierarchy from the perspective of their being lived as an object of quantum knowledge (the MAP system). But their becoming according to their status within knowledge goes through five identifiable stages. The three living things can be considered from four or five angles or ascending phases, from the empirical to the generic last-humanity or from the data of the lived to cloning, which is something else. These phases are those of their knowledge and distinguish themselves from every philosophical hierarchy. The data of the lived goes through several forms or stages of objectivity divided into two moments. First the moment of quantification itself, properly stated in five phases of these data, then in the second moment called generic or cloning through an indexing to the dimension of the Universe, aleatory subjects produced by quantification. These two orthogonal dimensions, horizontal quantification and vertical indexing, are obviously not those of an object in a Cartesian space, but those of ecological knowledge itself deployed in a non-standard fiction or eco-fiction space.

Let's start with the phases of matrix-based quantification of the lived. They are represented 1. either as in-themselves, as macroscopic and Newtonian, if you will, 2. as variables within the matrix or productive forces for the knowledge of life or as life's *forms of intuition*, 3. no longer as formal *a priori*, but as a *formal intuition* (Kant) and so determined. These quantum sort of *a priori* are forms of intuition that themselves become materiell and vectoriell, 4. always as these *a priori* but now grasped in their ultimate condition for reality, being "in-the-last-humanity," or as *a priori* under-determined under the generic condition of their indexation, 5. finally a completely different modality of the knowledge of life, a new reality that is no longer assumed to be individual in itself or the material prepared for the quantum experiment as above, but that which is its complementarity, the clone of this individual replaced and grasped now in its philosophical framework that is no longer reduced through its quantification, but is impoverished as a philosophical image. This is the symmetrical solution to the preceding problem.

1   *As empirical givens*. MAP are first of all simple entities of representation in-themselves, of the separable, localizable, and mixable givens, and at best correspond to a classical philosophy or a Newtonian state of the problem. The three types of living things, MAP, are the retroactively posited material and experience of a transcendental aesthetic. This is the place of the hierarchy of the living, of their war, and their excess.

2   *As variables, productive forces, or forms of the intuition of life.* Conjugating two by two within the matrix of life, the three living MAPs have become variables of the lived, man in particular is only one variable next to the others and without privileges. These are all properties of life's flux but treated retroactively from the matrix as lived productive forces of the future quantum knowledge of life. For there to be a universal and necessary science of life, a science modeled by the quantum and psychology, there must be a quasi-transcendental theoretical apparatus, that of superposition and the *a priori*.

The quantum—whose relationship with transcendental philosophy is known to be stretched but real—needs it.

3 *As formal intuition* and no longer as forms of intuition. For this science to become generic, neither philosophical nor positive, but participating through its variables of these two disciplines, it will be necessary to pass from properties as the formal *a priori* of intuition to the *a priori* as being a formal intuition constituted vectorially. They then form between them unequal inverse products, they are non-separable, non-localizable in a completely different sense than within representation. The two planes, that of philosophical representation of classical ecology and that of the matrix use of the *a priori*, cannot be cynically mixed. This transformation of factual givens into real non-formal *a priori* is the effect of the quantum matrix that retroacts on its givens and transforms them into simple variables without sufficiency. In one sense, in its quantum modeling, man does not have any exorbitant or metaphysical privilege even when it comes to life, he is an *a priori* of the lived like any other. With these variables conjugated, we obtain inverse products, MA (man as animalized) and AM (the animal humanized), but also MP and PM which form unequal and above all non-commutative products for the knowledge of life. The variables must be treated as not rigid and not formal *a priori*, *a priori* materials that are the forms proper to the vectoriell experience of the lived and through which the knowledge of life is given to us as a product.

4 *As generically under-determined a priori*. The *a priori* generally come in dualities or pairs, either space/time or wave/corpuscle. But the "transcendental" aesthetic that generally commands intuition, here of represented life, only requires, as we have known since Kant, that it surpass itself, and for this reason there is always a redoubling, the forms of intuition are here replaced by formal intuition, as we have just seen, the wave-corpuscle couple of the lived is unified by their equivalence. But this repetition is also a duplication of one of the opposite terms as variables. From there a possible indexing, either to philosophy through one form of cloning, or as here to the complex lived of superposition again. We must move to another level, equivalent to that of the transcendental imagination in its schematizing function. We will therefore soon have to pose the problem of a generic schematization, meaning idempotence (as originary generic unity) within vectoriality. And first examine this double indexing to the random subject or its double cloning, possible, generic, and epistemological.

Its Generic Indexing

Generic Cloning of the Aleatory Subject Through its Indexing to Reason-in-person or Lowering-over

The probable subject, once produced by the quantum or matrix process, has before it a possible double destiny depending on the double indexing that awaits it. Either that of the transcendental lowered-over by the imaginary number of Reason-in-person which works within the quantum, it remains within the immanence of the process and gives rise to the generic and under-determining subject as a clone. Or that of the transcendental raised-over by a transcendent support and one that works within philosophy, it comes out of quantum immanence and gives rise to an epistemological clone, which simulates the generic subject, a philosophical messiah. Let's start with its generic indexing to Reason-in-person.

The specifically ecological relationships between man/animal are no longer those of positive science, where they are facts of experience or givens for some mathematical parameter setting, nor those of philosophy as some inevitable context, but which no longer contributes partially and as a variable to their knowledge, they are first quantum or matrix-esque. A consequence of this thesis is that the animal within man and outside of man, one of the principal objects of vulgar ecology, now thought of by man with the partial assistance of philosophical definition for which the animal bears the burden if we at least measure it against the generic man who under-determines it.

The concept of the animal as a probable subject and then as a clone in a new and broader sense than the biological is very difficult to access even if it may be specifically ecological but generic in style. This can be explained if we understand the generic perspective as that of an experimental knowledge and not as a cynical conception of ecology so it is a transcendental and nonnaturalistic conception, knowledge being what essentially determines worldly and natural reality. Generic man as last-instance under-determines these understandings and guarantees their probability or their infinitely scientific openness. There are clones of living beings in the sense of biological cloning, but here, in this transcendental and nonempirical perspective, it is the animal in general as an animal/man fusion who is a "generic clone," meaning in the order of generic and non-philosophical understanding, of the probable subject as it is under-determined by it.

Man and animal are separately empirical models that can be adapted to each other, but only if each is isolated from the other or from their duality of fusion. On the other hand, in our conception of a non-standard ecology, it is their fusion itself that is the empirical model as a mixture, admittedly given first as philosophizable, but which must then be decomposed into its two variables, which implies its objectification by the matrix and its vectoriality. They are now fused as a single system and contribute to the carrying out of the last-instance. It is their system as it passes through different virtual states that effect it, the starting givens are a catalog of virtual possibilities, biological givens that are now prepared to be put into the form of state vectors.

Philosophy gives itself a subject and determines that subject by adding attributes, rational, political, linguistic, all transcendent: this means taking much from animals or depriving them of much. This accumulation of the capital of logos over man as their superior degree and as measure is the foundation for all philosophical or higher racism. On the other hand, the generic clone is built upon the probable and uncertain subject produced through the matrix, instead of being built upon the dogmatic subject, this is an addition of properties that are entirely subtracted from representation or that only add up within the abstract dimension of the matrix. But beyond the vectoriell matrix, which is necessarily one of the animal and man, the clone requires a parameter for its generic indexing. As the animal and man must share the terms of the fusion at a generic level, the one being the becoming-clone, the other being the constitutive parameter setting of the clone. With priority, man will assume the function of the transcendental or Universe index constitutive of the clone as generic and messianic, one cannot imagine the inverse order, the animal cannot be used for a parameter setting or as a generic measure for man who alone occupies Reason-in-person and its algebraic nature. The clone is therefore the animal who is within man and outside of man, but to which man has a generic relationship as last-instance. The old relations of the model are broken, those that came from Platonism as relations of paradigm and copies. The animal is no longer a simple subject with deficient predicates, but as an animal taken from the man/animal fusion, it becomes a kind of model in the now quasi-mathematical sense of a theory. It is no longer a source of facts which are the correlate of a determined theory, but a source of givens that can be spotted within a given parameter and that can be reprised by hypotheses issued by different disciplines. The clone that originates from the quantum does not respond speculatively to a model, this is a false symmetry that generic under-determination breaks. It is therefore a question of moving from the empirical or given mixture to its matrix-esque distribution into two variables for a subject = X, assuming moreover that that the subject = X can be given randomly as a human, so carrying algebra and the imaginary number, and this facing the other random outcome, that of the animal. But man must come out of the random process for the animal to have any chance of becoming a clone under-determined by generic indexing.

What now is the transformation of man as generic and its consequences for the animal? We are not reestablishing the ontologico-Aristotelian difference between soul and body, mind and body, a living and rational subject, which overlap with each other and are divided into each other. The structure of the generic matrix is univocally valid for the lived of the living, the only difference between them is that man has the power to think generically and to lay out the algebraic matrix, meaning to add an additional vector to that of nature in-itself. Does this reestablish an avatar of the old anthropo-logical cut? This cut is only valid for the clone, but it is still transformed and is no longer dominant. It being given that the generic is an understanding or a "truth," what is cloning? If the animal is within man and outside of man, it is necessary to find another cut between man = X and animality than philosophical difference, man is in some part devoid of animality and non-separable from it, this is an axiom devoid of empirical determinations and capable of under-determining them. Generic man as participating with the animal is also his own animal-clone, but a clone can be generic without being its own human clone. Generic man is an animal that has the power of truth because it has the power of fiction, but it is because he has the power of truth in-the-last-instance that he knows his affinity or proximity to the animal.

The subject = X that is yet inseparable from the animal is no longer a simple living thing who will return as the ultimate lived in the human as a non-individual form, but as a generic subject or as the last, "quasi" reflected, instance. Indeed, the problem remains that man alone can make generic theory, although the animal with its own culture obviously approaches it, but the understanding of this situation and its theoretical construction belongs only to the so-called generic man. The formula of "generic man" is dangerous and may lead us to believe in a new separated entity, while the human is also an animal or non-separated, and receives the "generic" attribute thanks only to the quantum and so therefore to algebra, which is the only attribute capable of separating it from human animality. Man and animal share culture, they could even share philosophy, but do not share the power of quantum physics. The animal is also related to itself or indexed to itself, but in the generic imaginary or algebraic mode that is of the human.

What distinguishes man in-the-last-instance from the animal is the power of the algebraic imagination. The acts of the last-instance must be conceived of as unclosed vectors, throws, or movements completed or summable in each instant but not as closed and in-itself. Only man can think = practice the generic. The animal, even the one within man, is thought under a generic condition uniquely in-the-last-instance, it is no longer an intra-rational cut in any sense. This is the only way to create a positive and human ecology, though anti-naturalist, the world of which is only the occasion and not the universal context. The animal is able to be measured neither with purely physical nature nor to the human being, so as deficient or sub-rational, we exclude these two correlative possibilities, they being philosophical interpretations. But the animal is able to be thought and measured by generic man at the same time as the animal must be protected from deterministic or realist capture, this being the way we defend the animal. Man-in-person extends into the animal-in-clone, but the generic defense of humans is extended by the defense of the animals. The clone is not a lesser human and the animal a sub-human, but it is under-determined in a generic manner, and this is a way of protecting it. As for man's philosophical servitude, it also extends to that of the animals, through the need to protect the weakest and through, it goes without saying, the struggle against capitalist sufficiency. This is the only way to link the defense of man and the defense of the animal as it is under-determined as a clone of the generic man and, especially as non-rational or rationally deficient, no longer that which would allow all superseding and equivocations in terms of the technical treatment. If we lower man away from the metaphysical toward generic man, it is inevitable that we drag the animal into this lowering, which is very particular since it is protective.

To quantify the man/animal mixture and its excesses of absolution and sufficiency is to liberate the dimension of ecological truth and fiction that comes back to human beings. The animal is no longer the model in the positive and scientific sense of man or his copy, nor inversely is man the paradigm of the animal. The meaning of model and copy must change. Generic man subtracts the animal from the use made of it by the despotic or sufficient individual, who reduces the animal to the state of a consumable object and abuses its sensible nature as a suffering animal.

The animal of eco-fiction, the one that we know in a "non-standard" way, is not an animal imaginarily projected by generic man, but a clone thought in-the-last-instance through him and whose mythical transcendence, which remains there despite everything, is lowered to the point of also possessing a generic generality, though it possesses it as an animal nature participating in the generic under-determination thus brought down to the scale of these lowered-over objects. Instead of reducing man to the level of a (rational) animal, the animal is reduced to the rank of the human's clone but as under-determined and so as non-naturalistic. Man and animal are not metaphysically reciprocated, which would cause them both to lose their respective privilege, and an ultimate noncommutativity is established between them, which is generally misunderstood as a humanism. Naturalist and cynical ecology is reversed here.

The animal as a philosophical clone is the residue derived from the mythic and metaphysical animal. But the principle of this ecology remains man as generic and not as a rational animal in-the-world, though he is that, but as a simple material for this generic ecology. Ecology is here futural and not overwhelmed by the weight of the past and the history of the world, it is perhaps an ecological fiction, a futural eco-fiction, once more a thought that is more adventural than adventurous.

The Epistemological Cloning of the Aleatory Subject Through its Being Indexed to Philosophical Reason: The Reversal of Cynical and Naturalist Ecology

Let's move on to indexing the random subject to philosophical reason. This is the complementary outcome, within the quantification of the lived, of the operation of the aleatory subject's indexing to superposition. How is it complementary? It is a way of actualizing Bohr's complementarity but at a more complex level of indexing, also explicitly involving philosophy and its traditional or raised-over transcendental. Of the possible double indexing of the aleatory subject, one is quantum and generic, before-first in our problematic, and the other is philosophical, complementary to the previous one, but only first by origin since the philosophical priority is subject to the quantum before-priority that formalizes it.

From the material of representation in-itself of the three living things themselves, which are *a priori* grasped as becoming-generic and through which life experiences itself and knows itself, we can distinguish yet another use of the living that is derived from the quantum and partially extra-quantic. No longer is it a question of deducing or under-determining a probable subject in the representation of living things through a classical and therefore random quantum process, but of deducing what becomes that probable subject taken directly as localizable *this time equally* in philosophy and not only within the enclosure of the quantum process. Through their being indexed this time to the classical philosophical transcendental, the quantum bifurcates and changes its destination, instead of becoming generic it becomes a philosophical repetition, drawing probable subjects from beings of a new type, that is "us, the MAP," random subjects who think of themselves as fallen straight from philosophy, even from theology, to which they are now indexed and which are in any case reflected within the mirror of philosophy. What they draw or subtract from our physico-biological being-represented and produce in this new indexing are what we will be calling, for want of anything better, the clones of human, animal, and plant *individuals*, clones of the three kinds of living things and no longer, as previously, the probable subjects produced on the basis of quantum knowledge. This is not a return to representation as supposed in-itself, it is a matter of another use of the quantum apparatus as a means of generating clones corresponding to the three givens of simple representation.

The process that begun as quantum bifurcates midway, at the crucial moment of understanding when the aleatory subject must choose between its being indexed to the transcendental of superposition as Reason-in-person, or that other more classical indexing to a philosophical transcendental, while moreover using the same *a priori* means. This is the final choice between lowered-over Reason-in-person with its messianic promise of an ecological life that opens and breaks the antinomy that enclosed it, and the philosophically overloaded reason that sinks into its own ruins because it returns within itself as a repetition of its own circle after a partially vain or unfinished detour through the quantum.

On this second co-lateral path, we therefore have material for three clones, depending on the three stases of the living, the clone derived from the material of the (animalized) man-animal represented or named "Man" who populates the cities, the clone derived from the (humanized) animal-man represented or named "Animal" who populates the earth, and finally the clone derived from the (humanized) plant-man and named "Plant" which populates the forests. These entities envelop the probable subjects, though indexed from now on to philosophy and no longer to the transcendental nature of superposition.

The theoretical interest in cloning obviously resides in the ambiguity of its two forms of the transcendental: quantum and lowered-over (paradoxically) by superposition and philosophical or raised-over by over-determination. To put it in other terms as the possible confusion between two kinds of unity-identity, which are idempotence and the synthetic-originary that are said to be the apperception of the lived. Instead of forming, as before, the generic lived that would take them out of philosophy, the second returns to its fold and forms the old circle. In this form and with this circular and vicious genealogy, these are now clones as images of the living, deprived of macroscopic properties, though this time incompletely, which have simple been damaged instead of quantified, and which are spontaneously attributed to them in everyday life and by common sense. This means that they do not correspond exactly to the living as received by philosophy and common sense, nor to the data prepared as superposed quantum systems. Clones are collateral avatars of probable subjects and came down almost straight from philosophy. Not quite though, they were diverted so that they are finally reoriented by philosophy and "brought back to the right path." This is the path that brings the particles back to the older way of atomism as an anthropocentric residue whose "propensity" is known, the tendency to deviate or fall by drifting along. Atomism is a philosophical, and therefore anticipated, version of quantum thought which had not yet happened. But we already know about this retroactive genealogy.

This deduction should make possible an experimental verification of "quantum ecology" in an almost inverse form to the previous one. Clones are an example of a confusion that is always possible between a rigorous transcendental understanding or quantum of the lived by itself and its apparent or philosophical understanding as a circle of "life." This genealogy of the philosophical appearance of the animal or human as such is a trait that belongs to the status of clones. This is why man and animal end up in philosophy by being models for each other. The positive science of biology encompasses both concepts with some adjustments or fine-tuning of the givens. So that philosophy and biology have a tendency to erase differences and to reabsorb Being-in-the-last-humanity or erase it in an asymptomatic vision, to efface it in a monism of animality or life "in general" that usurps and denies the function of the in-the-last-lived. The ethical dimension of ecology maintains the break of symmetry between humans and the rest of the living. Without saying that man is or is not an empire within an empire, ethics requires the refusal of this naturalism. We will set out some rules to this end.

Marx, Nietzsche, and Foucault; Or, the Generic Without the Quantum

The solutions given by Marx and Nietzsche are philosophical rather than quantum and cannot save us from the antinomy. M and A are treated as mixed empirical properties and fused in a philosophical manner with an undetermined result, which can lead toward a redoubling as a man or as an animal. If it is toward the animal, we have a naturalist vision or if it is toward humans, we have a humanist vision. This is the philosophical solution with two symmetrical outcomes or inclinations. The antinomy's philosophical solution is therefore a complex biological result, if not a confusing one. This solution remains within the circle of philosophy as a physical ecology with a Newtonian obedience. Nietzsche's Platonic reversal also led to an animal revolution of the body, but not truly to the non-commutative products of the variables. The Nietzschean bridge from the animal-man to the overhuman is necessarily still an animal-human or a superior human-animal. This is always the philosophical solution for bestiality, a forceful movement or one through transcendence, an over-determination, what we have called "philosophy's greater racism."

The two possible and inverse products are, on the other hand, found again within the matrix in a different form than that of commutative philosophy, man and animal are now the two variables of a subject = generic X which can support either human or animal relationships, they are no longer combinable properties within philosophy itself in the mode of blending. From this point of view, quantum algebra is missing in Nietzsche just as it is in Marx, their solution is purely philosophical. It would have been necessary for the matrix setting to signify the intervention of the imaginary number and consequently that it is this number that acts with and on the side of man without being for that a humanism. The humanity of the in-the-last-instance is not grounded upon a humanism despite certain appearances owing to the last-instance—far from being an ordinary metaphysical causality—being an under-determination of humanist sufficiency as well as animal sufficiency and the Nietzschean reversal of the animal as overhuman. Nietzsche also thinks through the inseparable doublet and antinomy of the "passage" but as reaffirmation or superhumanity. He too, like Marx, lacks the quantum.

We are instead looking for the under-affirmation of this human-animal. Man and animal must be treated as independent variables conjugated in a non-commutative way, this time with an indexing to the dimension of the Universe which gives the lived its lowered-over transcendence, not indexed to man or to the animal, this is the messianic achievement of the quantum, not a biological point of view but an epistemological one. Matrix setting and then indexing signify the intervention of the imaginary number that acts alongside of man without however giving rise to a humanism.

It is only from the point of view of the under-determining last-instance (which again is not a biological point of view but an epistemological one) that M, A, P have functions or "differences of nature" which refuse the diffusion of the lived, and particularly the human lived, into the transcendence of life. The absence of a metaphysical nature prevents the epistemological distinction from diffusing into the spectrum of differences of degree that it under-determines.

The MAP model is made of separate Aristotelian macroscopic entities, it becomes mechanically Cartesian and dynamically Newtonian. Marx tried to break this localization with his principle that man is a physical being that makes nature human. This is still a vicious circle (hence a possible Aristotelian rootedness from Feuerbach's generic) because it reasons with separate macroscopic terms instead of breaking with this way of thinking through the positing of a quantum or lived man/animal non-separability, which would make it possible to define a generic man or also applicable in-the-last-instance, as lived, for the animal and the plant that man is as well. And a generic animal but only in-the-last-instance, through the human traits that it contains.

Marx's insufficiency is not to *think* quantumly, barely touching the generic which remains "Feuerbachian." He does not define something indivisible, that is a quantum of humanity in the form of a complex matrix-esque non-separability, but immediately moves on to indexing, whereas if he had passed through the quantum he could only index man/animal as last-instance on the basis of the imaginary number.

Basically, the generic is easy and spontaneous— especially in this Feuerbachian context which constantly guides it—if it is not conditioned by the matrix form of non-separability. It is necessary that philosophy and the quantum be two extreme dimensions of a matrix or the two properties of a subject = X which does not form simple doublets, that these two dimensions are nevertheless non-separable without being specular or unified in a commutative way like transcendence within the One-of-sufficiency. The complete quantum of humanity links the two dimensions (vectorialization and indexing) that form a complex generic matrix.

Marx's axiom (concerning man as a natural being who makes nature human) is therefore generic in a Feuerbachian and purely philosophical sense because it lacks the quantum structure as matrix and imaginary. For him "making physical man human" is to index man to an individual transcendental quasi-subject. Unless we consider the superposition of the imaginary number as a relation of production (RP) in Marx's sense, which is not impossible, but it is precisely on this delicate point that we must clearly separate ourselves from Marx and his RP which conserve a certain philosophical ambiguity even in the last-instance. Marx allows for the psychological and willful human as RP rather than as PF (productive forces). But generic science requires that there are two subjects, the one who is caught in the double philosophical transcendence is that of Marx's RP, and the generic one whose form is quantum, immanental, and through superposition, is the last-instance. Man is PF undoubtedly through philosophy, but mainly through science, so this is not a theological redoubling of/within philosophy. Marx seems to throw out everything that is subjectively human and cast it into the superstructure, he retains something of bourgeois, psychological, and voluntary subjectivism. But in its aspect as superposed imaginary number, nature can be seen as quasi-human, this time as a subject of-the-last-instance that physical science tolerates. It is nature made human but which remains nature or physical within man. Make nature human? "Human" is not here an adjective related to the subject "nature." Fusion or superposition of nature and man, the human subject is capable of humanity and naturalness, of acts of thought and acts that are purely physical or that are understood as physical. It is a not a Spinoza-esque parallelism between attributes, but a quantum superposition with an infinity of attributes or "Feynman's paths" that interfere. As a mechanistic thinker, Spinoza thinks of bodies as relationships of speed and slowness, or as their proportion, but as generic and quantum we think them as relations of philosophy and science, relations whose proportions come under the imaginary number. They are not exactly correlations, they are uni-lations, unilateral dualities, or relations grounded in a without-relation that is nothing but the One as without-relation of superposition. What does "immediate unity" mean? Certainly not that the whole is within the whole, but at least the complementarity of a duality that is "one" or continues moreover as "two" in-one. This is the non-relation of the vector or the wave and the particle that is related to it.

The Marxian axiom of nature made human is an attempt to define a generic style of the quantum of humanity but it is the properly quantum aspect that is not developed, Marx obviously does not have the quantum at his disposal. To compensate for this absence, the immediate unity of man and nature must not be interpreted dialectically or in a Feuerbachian way, precisely because it is immediate. Here too, these are two indeterminate terms that can undoubtedly be determined linguistically, but they will be treated instead according to a formalism as variables intended to (under-)determine generic man.

"Rational animal" is an Aristotelian formula, but what matters is the superior treatment of this formula, which no longer necessarily makes it a definition or even an axiom. Traditionally this formula, in reality a doublet, reflects itself especially if it is philosophical and not a scientific-positive statement or some other doxa below philosophy. But for man = X, we can also conjugate the two properties, variables, or predicates that the physical animal and reason are. Put in this way as a matrix, the subject = X—which is substituted for "rational man" whose quantum transformation is marked by probability—is the phenomenon targeted by the inverse products of the physical animal and reason, as these products are indexed to the imaginary number. This is the precession of the matrix's orientation, while its first intervention as a quantum variable is just that of one property next to another and not yet the matrix's orientation.

We therefore distinguish between the subject/predicate identification, which has become the Möbius strip like torsion of the animal-as-rational (Deleuze), and their generic superposition, which is still another thing. It requires distinguishing the rational-animal as a real object superposed and able to be quantumly constructed with vectors, and the rational-animal as an object philosophically given to be known as a result of a random or probable process of understanding. The old "rational animal" has now become the generic subject = X capable of properties of the lived or of life, and properties or rational acts, but it is no longer exhausting itself in those properties that under-determine it.

CONCLUSION
ETHICS BETWEEN ECOLOGY AND MESSIANITY

The Ecological Amplitude of Ethics

The introduction into thought of ecology as material and as thought gives ethics a new amplitude beyond its rationalist closure and Judaic openness. We are not attempting to subject moribund and harassed ethics to what announces itself in the characteristics of ecology and so instead of subjecting ecology to what is left of ethics and attempting a new mixture, which is the usual way of dealing with the antinomy, we are attempting to make them work together in a non-dialectical entanglement.

In an intense ecological environment, ethics can no longer be satisfied with its objectives being set at the level of philosophizing humans through the elimination of the animal and the plant, or even the Earth that they inhabit and exploit as passive occasions for their applications. All this material, this "matter" of ethics as Kant would say, has been greatly enriched since rationalism, but above all we must consider it as co-determining, not only mixed but also "entangled" (although it is not in a dialectical form, as Hegel objected to Kant) with the form of its principles and rules.

What we have called above Reason-in-person is the principle of superposition in its complex and vectoriell nature, in a state of collapse or ruin, so as to strip it of its showy old clothes or multicolored philosophical rags that are only worthy of attracting flies, wasps, and other flying philosophers, and precisely contributed to the confusion of Reason-in-person with those materials that becomes its masks, so this name was a way of returning it to its quantum nudity and weakness. However, if superposition is pure reason, its purity is not unrelated to its materials, it is simply not mixed with them, they have the formal purity of the coefficient, if not that of the imaginary number. It is simply not combined or mixed, only entangled with them according to relationships that never end in confused mixtures but in entanglements that form the object of a process of knowledge.

But this universal extension of the principle of superposition cannot be held within the limits of philosophical Being-in-the-world, neither by Being or by the world, as the Greeks would have liked, or like we find with the Stoics and the other authors of projects of universal concord with the world or with . . . the moon. This extension, measured in a Copernican way, is both materially too limited and too vast because the subject of ethics remains a philosophical subject limited internally and externally. Not only is the entanglement of ethics with matter more extended and smaller than the World, going from the particle to the corpuscle through all the possible degrees, but it is under-determined by a subject who can no longer belong to the macroscopic world alone. Our thesis is that ecology, as a way of thinking rather than of eating, of traveling messianically rather than simply living, sketches a new way for humans, one that goes from their withdrawal or subtraction from the Earth to the Universe, which is the correlate of this subtraction. Between the two, which are two ways of exceeding the average dimension of the World, from their withdrawal to the greatest dimension of the Universe, men only inhabit locally so as to travel or extend their journey with some rest, to carry along the plant on their journey, that plant which is always likely to fix itself to the ground like humans do to the sky or in their cave. In the World and outside of the World? In the World because outside the World anyway . . . and in the Universe. Humans travel within a space that is always defined by two heterogenous dimensions which are themselves double—the World where horizontality dominates verticality, and the Universe where verticality dominates horizontality—and these communicate only at a central point that is for a new and second time the World, but in a World that deepens or disappears "into" the below and rises "from" the below, and multiples in itself within all its dimensions like a holographic object. The World is only stasis or the point of intersection for all these journeys that assume every dimension. The span or amplitude of ethics is this purely rational or transcendental dimension, co-traced by the quantum between the generic subject and superposition that the probable subject, resulting from the quantum treatment, is indexed to. It is necessary to move the circle of philosophy or the World toward the quantumly modeled opening of the Universe and not through philosophy fixed to the World, to a World entirely on the surface and without real depth.

Like Kant, we also have our three objects for the "dialectical" or "quantum" transcendental. We will not believe that the extension grows in an apparently cosmological way from one to the other. It would instead be the inverse, more exactly the height of lowered philosophy, the metaphysical palace collapses on itself into its lowest depths, the dregs, where generic man lives. It seems urgent that the fundamental human affect be recovered under sentimental ecology and its correlative universal dimension beyond the positive sciences devoted to it. This urgency is confused, without any certainty of success, with the transformation of the cynicism and vulgarity of its time, under rigorous and human conditions of thought.

In identifying this collapse of the lived that constitutes the aleatory subject quantumly produced, we have symmetrically identified the entity capable of responding to this collapse, the generic clone, such as it fulfills, through its indexing to the dimension of the Universe, this quasi-seismic gap dug into the world of representation. This duality that the probable subject forms with the universe and which is resolved as the-last-instance, is constructed by us as a new "imaginary" bridge, one which Nietzsche did not generically project from the bottom of the collapse so as to spread it into the Universe. He preferred to follow the path of philosophy and throw the unitary arch between the animalized pre-human and overhuman, and did not succeed in overcoming, no more than Marx, the man/animal duality to move toward a quantum conception of man. This new kind of bridge would require, according to its utopian architecture, new engineers and architects supporting the future, formed at least in physics, but necessarily so, as well as in philosophy, and capable of projecting, from the bottom of the collapse or from below the sky, a single messianic arch that merges at its departure with the clone that assumes it, and at its other extreme, with the Universe as an uncertain and suspended pillar into the void where it is lost. The Nietzschean tightrope walker lacking messianity still was advancing on his two feet, dancing on a single bridge with a thousand arches, he was only a wide-awake semi-sleepwalker . . .

Affective Monism and Messianic Amplitude

Without underestimating the importance of the lived as effective, we do not defend in any particular way an attitude of empathy or compassion, even pity for a finite life, or even for an infinite life though it be crushed by itself in the same way as the infinite crushing of the transcendental egological immanence (M. Henry) proper to the excess of the divine. However, affectivity is only one of the possible variables. Correlatively, the nonhuman animal remains at the border of language, it cannot think algebraically, admit the ruin or collapse of its transcendence, or make an ethical decision. Ecology often bases its decisions and behaviors on this affective monism. The sole affectivity that underlies most "animal" or "wildlife" ethics is not enough, it must be conjugated and related to the probable human subject capable of making "algebraic" decisions. To be the guardian of the living in their lived experience it is necessary that one of these living things be its own guardian and be able to extend ethics beyond its sphere. Only a very particular animal, capable of idempotence because of its very complexity, can emerge from the affective monism that deprives it of any ethical and messianic amplitude, and conjugate it with its other variable, the knowledge that we now know belongs to it as much as to the affectivity of the lived. How, in these conditions, can we establish an ethics that can, without contradiction, agree to take charge of all living things in being unburdened of them, except for being the bearer of this added function of the last-instance, who carries his exceptional trait to the level of the only universality that neither has an exception nor a privilege since it is that of the Universe that responds to the collapse of all responsibility. Life and the lived are housed not as beings within Being, but only as the lived within the Universe. The indexing of the lived to the Universe replaces the traditional ontological difference of philosophy with generic difference and sets the lived and the Universe in relation through the mediation of the quantum. We need the plane of thought that is appropriate to ecology to make it glide or move away from Being or the World into the Universe and from beings to the lived-without-life. To refuse this "displacement" is to return to or to prolong the antinomy of ecology and philosophy, which is a contradiction of and in ontology, this is the change of terrain necessary to think philosophy ecologically. Ecology is not an ontological object; it is a reform of philosophy by a new science. The lived/Universe correlation is the axis of a new science, but not in the sense of a modality of traditional philosophy. Nietzsche put his finger on the problem of confusing Being with life and declaring that the ground of Being or its true concept is that of life. Nietzsche, however, refashioned a philosophy of life and gave it the image of Being. We interpret life as non-philosophy; we are in the *ecological age of philosophy*.

The Conjugation of Ecology and Ethics

The non-locality and non-separability of the lived man/animal/ plant system, conjugated with the subtractive separability of the last-instance, are the traits of ethical acts within an immanent ecological context. This is not a metaphysical hierarchy of means/ends or the system of four causes. This does not mean absolute equality of treatment between living things. If man is a part of nature that makes nature human, ethics is finally entangled with ecology in the depths of man as a natural being as well. But this does not mean erasing all distinction between them or making this distinction a gap or a chôra, only a collapse, the quantum modeling of ecology prohibits these extreme solutions or conjugates them conventionally. This means finally putting ethics in-the-last-human-instance at least in the service of nature, a nature from which it cannot be separated except within metaphysics, but the quantum prohibits all traditional metaphysics.

It should also be taken into account that this ethico-ecological comportment is not a decision or an event but an opaque or probable process. But can ethics be probable instead of dogmatic, as it naturally tends to be? If there is a higher ethics, a supreme principle for ethical rules themselves, it amounts to protecting human living beings as "in-the-last-humanity" or as a power to under-determine rationalist ethics and other sorts that are all based upon philosophical sufficiency, which cannot do justice to the animal, the plant, and even less so to human beings. The ethics capable of lowering them or imposing the quantum collapse of the in-the-last-humanity is immanent to non-standard thought or, to put it too quickly, "non-ecological" thought.

However, this non-ecological ethics has probable effects, not dogmatic, imperative, or categorical results, because its decisions or behaviors are entangled, although never as solid and determined. Probable or aleatory ethics and provisional ethics in the absence of any certainty are not the same. What does the formula of the animal within man and outside of man mean? Is it like Kant's "in the world and outside of the world"? This last formula indicates a generic universality that runs through man beyond Being-in-the-world along an axis of indexation. But we can't say that man is in the animal and outside of the animal, unless all these inclusions and exclusions are remodeled according to the animal as a reference, but the non-separability that is unilateral or in-the-last-instance is not reversible. It is a matter of humanizing the already animalized man, and not animalizing man a little more as a Nietzschean overanimal/overman. The aleatory subject receives its original matrix-esque or vectoriell complexity and then, through his being indexed to the Universe, a non-animalizable supplement of humanity that augments his productive ethical forces of degrowth and his power to weaken or under-determine his violence.

This ethics is ecological only through its object, the World it affects as a circle, or the absolute place that insufficiently shifts to make room for humans. But it aims to reorient man away from his interest for the World toward generic man who has the opening onto the wide openness of the Universe as a correlate and who allows a truly ethical intention, meaning one indexed humanly to the Universe. The three axioms cited earlier are effects of universe-orientation and not of Being-in-the-World, from their in-the-last-humanity they pierce through the cosmic wall that stands against it and blocks the Universe.

Let us return to the question: what is the generic transformation of man and the animal now? The ontologico-Aristotelian difference between soul and body, mind and body, living and rational subject, which overlap and share in each other, is still not reestablished. The structure of the generic matrix is univocally valid for man and the animal, the only difference between them is that man has the power to think generically by combining abstract vectorialization and indexing, to add an additional vector by idempotence to those they manipulate as well as with quantum indexing. So, we ask again, does this restore an avatar of the old anthropo-logical cut? It is transformed into a simple material and is no longer dominant. The generic cut is simply idempotent, man and animal have the same structure of the lived, man simply has the power to think vectorially and add the sum of vectors to them, to sum them up and index them. Man and animal share culture, they could even share philosophy, but still not quantum physics. The generic subject is an animal that "has" the power of truth, but more profoundly this is because it has the power of the truth but in-the-last-instance so that it knows its affinity or proximity with the animal, which is its clone state. While, as we have said, philosophy gives itself a subject and determines it by adding attributes like rational, political, linguistic, all transcendent, it takes them away from the animals or deprives them of it, takes this accumulation as their measure. This too is part of the foundation of any philosophical or greater racism, the clone is built on the aleatory subject, it is an addition of properties that are subtracted on the whole from human representation or that only add up in the dimension of the infrastructure. As under-determined clone, the animal is like a schema or mediation that allows the passage from the lived vectoriell infrastructure to the superstructure or instead from the human or before-priority aleatory subject to the supposed man/animal in itself. The man-of-the-last-instance is therefore, as man-animal, the material model for the animal who is his clone.

Generic Ecology's Ethical Rules and the Critique of Vulgar and Philosophical Ecology

Common or vulgar ecology contains a small dose of explicit philosophy, but implicitly all the more. Ecological beliefs have taken over from theological ones, we see within the earth and on this earth our hell and our heaven together. If we amplify or maximize this dose, it is not to satisfy a secret desire that would substitute it as a new theology in place of the old one in order to serve a consumerist and materialistic humanity, offering our anguish a new salvation or possibility for an accessible survival through our technology. Our objective is quite different, it is to clearly define the adversary because there is one marked out for us albeit in a confusing way. These are some of the consequences and ethical rules that we draw from the generic properties, not of life in-itself, but from the knowledge of life by itself and determined by the lived of-the-last-instance. We seek them by taking Kant's three formulas as our guiding formula, quasi-mathematical formulas that are schemas for experience. We would have approximately the following formulas, which are theoretical imperatives with ethical value.

1 The first imperative is that of the quantum abstraction of the lived-without-life and of the vectoriell formalism that strikes MAP as variables and PF. It fashions the living *a priori* as undifferentiated and extends the generic from M to AP. It says that you will not treat the three MAP entities as separated and/or mixed orders in a rationally transcendent way. Their non-separability is not that of represented entities or entities in-themselves (in a hierarchy of infinite problems) but of vectors. So it is no longer a question of equal treatment between MAP as between representable living instances.

2 There are no privileges or exceptions in nature from a scientific point of view, but a fundamental equality whose abstraction is not raised by the philosophical concept. Ordinary ecology is obsessed with the exception and the ideological struggle against the exception, if need be it is positively scientific but then it can only declare itself against man or to secretly despise man. Generic ecology is not based unilaterally on philosophy alone or on biology and chemistry alone, it is the conjugation of these two sources, a quantumly formalized conjugation but under-determined above all by the lived of the in-the-last-humanity. Its problem is not one of replacing philosophy, but here again of making the best use of philosophy, the least authoritarian one, for the human beings that have created it. Humans are in-the-last-instance only on the condition that they are not exceptions. As a man in-the-last-humanity, you will not make an exception of yourself or of others.

This is a quantum limitation for any spontaneous ecology, at once vulgar and philosophical, and especially for the bad equality of ecological pathos. In this perspective we must review the concept of human "dignity" as opposed to man's "worth" (Kant) and "value" (Nietzsche), from now on solely based upon the lived in-the-last-humanity. The animal within the "common" man is comparable to the animal full stop, but this is not the animal according to man understood by him as in-the-last-humanity. The animal in the common man is an occasion for generically humanizing. From this point of view, which is still elementary, we can distinguish the animal and the plant 1. as living things in-themselves, 2. as able to be biologically placed in man from whom they cannot be separated, 3. finally as thinkable according to the in-the-last-humanity. We are trying to go beyond the first two points of view, which are those of philosophical ecology, with the third which will require a revision of the first two.

3   Quantum-generic representation requires *entanglement without mixture*, the non-separability of the human subject undoubtedly, but different from between-oneself, from the between-each, and between-all, since these notions refer to transcendent mixtures rather than to an immanence of lived entanglements. This is the "schema" that gives algebraic and idempotent meaning to MAP relations, not to think separately and locally about human "kind" and animal "kind" (or species). A vector is not external to a first vector but prolongs it and adds itself with it, the addition is a discreet extension, which corresponds to the animal within man and outside of man, but what is outside of man is either an animal occasion to be humanized or already humanized and becoming immanent. Linearity is not an introjection of the animal into man, of living entities into one another. The relationships of MAP, and in particular of A which is within M, are not localized but entangled without mixture. There is a linearity of entities in a common or generic cosmos, but no divine localization of man

as an intelligible or divine being (except to make him the bearer of an assumed divine logic), no empire in an empire, no dominant state in the society of the lived unlike that of the living, yet this one is able to be transformed by the in-the-last-humanity which, without being an exception, does not simply number among the rest of the living.

4 The living are lived projects or vectors (even the plant), not things or substances. There is no primary or empirico-worldly ecological objectivity, but summations on the flux of a quantum objectivation that remains immanent, a vectoriality deeper than the difference between ends and means, of worth and dignity, and other divisions. These entities are completed at every moment but not closed in and for themselves, they are instead unifacial and open, without any objective transcendence of the philosophical sort. This is therefore unilaterality without specular doublets, the living are vectors, not identities closed on themselves, ecstatic entities if need be, but whose exstasis has been stopped as in the case of the plant which is an exstasis that is becoming very slowly, on the verge of stopping, and of the contemplation of the world if not the universe as if the universe had dug the plant down into the ground.

5 Non-separability could lead us to believe in an identity but it is an appearance, holism is indivisibility rather than totality. There are only discreet transfinite flows or unilateralities. Unilaterality is not a doublet but a supplementarity, it is an effort to undo the doublets and circles through the subtraction of the "without" (humaniziation-without-humanism) but the subtraction itself is not absolute or through the void it allows a unilaterality, an achievement without closure to persist.

Vectoriell or lived and complex humanity transcends only through its idempotence, in such a way that one could call it algebraic and "proto"-rational. Humanization in-the-last-instance immanentizes ends and means without these being based any longer in the World. The lived, even more than life, is precisely an effort by humanity to subtract itself from its insertion into the circles of the cosmos, from the grasp of the horizon, from "man in the world" or from "Being-in-the-world." In the world, we are already too much. No more in the unconscious because the unconscious is man overwhelmed by God this time. The ultimate lived does not give rise to a moral Platonism coupled with a rootedness in life's facticity.

6   Noncommutativity is the refusal or impossibility of exchanging the lived for any other, no equivalent reversible permutation in the inverted conjugations between MAP, except confusion and the appearance of the in-itself. True equality is the world of the "in-the-last-humanity" against abstract egalitarianism. Does the generic reinforce the human exception? Human dignity is not an exception but a givenness and a transmission. At the same time, it completes the knowledge of life's orientation toward precisely a dignity of the lived-in-the-last-humanity, and tears it away from the representative reason of philosophy.

7   Is it a question of practicing a purely defensive generic ecology against the likes of the capitalist economy's assaults and against the philosophy that is its way of knowing? Defensive, in any case, as common ecology always has been, but we limit ourselves to changing its theoretical bases and reformulating more positively its problems and its prohibitions by drawing all the consequences from its lived determination in-the-last-humanity.

8   Mathematical symmetry of life and the living are replaced by the project as a generic tendency in the transfinite symmetry of the lived. If there is symmetry, it is not reducible to either vectoriell infrastructure or to superstructural idempotence. It only serves in some indirect schematization or symmetrical

becoming as an immanent and messianic tendency of humanity toward itself rather than toward a divine state. There is a final or second symmetry between the matrix-esque basis and the immanental real of the in-the-last-humanity. Non-standard knowledge is a symmetrical becoming, not a rigid structure. Schematism would be symmetry through mediation, which is contrary to the position of the mediated-without-mediation as last-instance and under-determination preventing the reversibility of causality that is necessary within symmetry. How then should we interpret the final symmetry of the generic despite the irreducible and transfinite occasional givenness? The secret of symmetry is not in being final or in becoming rather than in being an object or structure, but of being only in-the-last-humanity. Messianity is more than the correlate, it is the hope that fashions the in-the-last-humanity.

The Before-first Defense of Man and the First Defense of the Animal

A distinction is made between an absolute ethics of philosophical inspiration and a generic ethics which conjugates science and philosophy in equal parts into a single messianity. We refuse the first, which is objective and positivist, ecology molded to itself and its sufficiency, a consumer of philosophy and so self-contradictory, that of philosophical or natural environments, funds, and stocks, which can be exploited at will. We set it against a "subjective" or fundamentally human ecology. It is subtracted by the generic in which the animal and the other goods are no longer (to take up an old conceptuality) in themselves, but rather for themselves out of step in relation to themselves. The generic is not, however, the individual or Sartrean for-itself, it is in-the-last-instance and under-determining for that same reason. The generic combines the fundamental Marxian concept of determination in-the-last-instance and the subtractive effect of the imaginary number.

If generic ethics rejects statistical mixtures, nuances, and especially the absolute aspiration that goes with philosophy's self-affirmation (however, it takes into account a principle uncertainty), it tolerates being probabilistic in a quantum way rather than a statistical one. We have to conclude that all it can do is defend humans in-the-last-instance and defend animals and plants in the second position. The experimental and uncertain character destroys the risk of a vicious circle and the sufficiency of auto-defense or sufficiency that supports positivist ecology. Left to itself, philosophy does not succeed in freeing itself from this principle of Sufficient Ecology.

This liberation is a process, the ethical degrowth of philosophy is only a work of defense or protection in nature, not a work of condemnation or moral imperatives, of transcendent commands directly related to one another, front against front. This ethics is essentially indirect. Defending the living means that they will be defended by themselves, but in-the-last-instance or indirectly, it is not an immediate self-defense.

It involves the lowering, the internal collapse of non-sufficient transcendence. Collapse is a co-lapse, a shift from a violent philosophical transcendence to another whose collapse allows access to the generic real.

But ethics does not only aim at the uncertain or probable defense of animals and, as before-priority, the generic defense of man, it must make human that animal within man and outside of man. To make human is first to treat man as the in-the-last-instance. As a generic clone, not in the biological or specular sense, not one for technological transhumanism or overhumanism. In the wake of biologism, the subject as clone is too often reduced to being just a coat rack holding up prosthetic technologies, this is not the clone in-the-last-humanity of the animal within man and outside of him. The generic clone simply signifies that the animal must be treated humanly *at least in-the-last-instance, which means indirectly.* Cloning here does not concern physical nature or a man/animal mixture, it is a matter of a treatment by indexing and not by essence. Instead of treating the animal as an anthropologically deficient animal in-itself, we will treat it as a human caught in its collapse of-the-last-instance. The aim here is to avoid confusion between the animal deficient in logos, a deficiency thought of in a philosophical context, and the collapse of the lived, which is a quantum phenomenon. The subject = X will thus return to Reason-in-person or to superposition in a non-individual form, but as a quasi-reflective generic subject, and yet it will be inseparable from the animal. Should we also say that the animal is the clone of generic man alone or that the animal is taken as under-determined by the animal/man in terms of its mixtures as well as its material? In this case, man would also be a clone but under-determining/determined. Both statements are random and possible in the differently distended philosophical circle. But in any case, cloning responds to a second measure of experimental and probable logic, it must have been realized, it cannot be predicted *a priori* as philosophy claims.

The legitimate treatment of the animal as a source of givens for man himself in the biological sciences is not directly derived from their treatment as under-determined clone in-the-last-instance, although this derivation is always possible or interesting, albeit contingent. Generic ecology cannot be used to ground that ordinary positive ecology in which the animal serves, within certain limits, as a model for the knowledge of man, but only as an animal, because man adds an irreducible function that is specific to the animal whose positive knowledge does not need to be grounded. This is the only way to link the defense of the animal to the defense of man as it is under-determined as the clone of generic man and especially no longer as the rational or rationally deficient animal, which authorizes all supersessions [*dépassements*] and equivocations in their technical treatment. If we make man fall from metaphysics toward generic man, it is inevitable that we will drag the animal into this lowering, but this is the only way to ensure that the animal's defense will be equal to that of man's, meaning in the second order or the priority that suits the animal.

Even for this environment of knowledges as a new nature or ecumene where ecological finitude remains, there is a positive appropriation problem that rejoins philosophy's classical objectives. The before-first defense of generic man is also an appropriation of the good relation to this new nature. Defense is a positive act, the reduction of transcendence, not its negation, but the repetition that lowers it from its under-determining root. This is a positive ethics if it is not a simple negation of evil, a dialectical opposition, it consists less in removing or subtracting its means from domination than in inventing another use for defense. Within this ethical order, everything must be asked of man and nothing of the animal, except for the animal who is within man and under his guidance, not simply as separated under his protection and which only requires to be trained by him. Ethics is not for the animal in-itself who needs it but cannot provide it by itself, let alone is it the hermeneutical concern for self, this is its weakness. The acts of ethical safeguarding will be formulated concretely according to three axioms (safeguarding humans, the least suffering for the animal, the moderated use for the plant) but the three axioms regulate the relationship of conflict or collision between humans and animals according to the principle that man is an animal that makes the animal human, this is the generic meaning or orientation. This transformation implies a process, cloning is a knowledge or a "truth."

The only way to establish a human, but anti-naturalist ecology, and one whose world is only occasion and not a uni-versal context, is first of all to refuse the ecology of the in-itself environments, philosophical or natural, in order to ground ecology upon the generic in which the animal is thought not as in-itself but as a clone drawn from and under-determined, but secondly, meaning a priority of the philosophical kind, by generic man, *that other clone*, which is a clone of messianic before-priority of the in-the-last-instance. What then distinguishes these two types of clones, man and animal, how is this difference in the types of priorities realized? Four conditions have to be met in order for man to be able think = practice the generic and in it the operation of cloning in its two forms, either generic or before-priority or human, or generic in terms of the priority proper to the animal, 1. as the simple lived-without-life common to all living things, 2. the control of the algebraic or the complex and the imaginary, 3. an indexing to and a cloning in superposition as a form of the Universe, 4. the aleatory duality of subjects that emerge from the quantum process, either as a (humanized) animal or as an (animalized) human.

If man/animal are two properties or variables, the subject = X differs from them as its two possible states. This is no longer the subject-predicate or animal-logos relationship. There is a possible inversion of these non-commutative products. The empirical model or the one providing the givens (and not facts) to be put into perspective can no longer be the simple animal, but must be the man-animal. So that now it is this fusion that is the empirical model treated with philosophy or the quantum as an index. The empirical model was already treated in positive scientific biology, but it is from now on the man-animal system that is the central support or the subject as passing through different states that virtually carry it out. The system as a catalog of virtual possibilities, of initial scientifico-biological givens, is from now on that of the prepared givens of the system to be put in the form of vectors, for example the Aristotelian figures that will be considered and treated as state vectors. We must take into account the random exit of potentialities that constitute the lived, either the human lived or the animal lived. Hence cloning doubles itself.

The animal and man separately are then thought of as a generic clone in-the-last-instance, and it is no longer anyway an intra-rational cut. We can no longer say that animals can be measured in the World as a simple and specifically biological life, nor that they can be measured by human being, and therefore as deficient or sub-rational, we exclude these two correlative possibilities that come from philosophical interpretation, except that they are thinkable and measurable by the generic clone in the messianic of before-priority. The ecological animal or the one treated as such must be thought of as a second priority clone and not as an animal in-itself. The clone is not made equal with man who is generic and is thought of messianically as before-priority, but it is protected and defended from being gripped as deterministic and realist as well as dominated and exploited by it, a defense and exploitation based upon its weakness as a philosophically dominant clone.

The generic defense is in two degrees, or two types; the defense of human beings, which must take into account their aleatory or problematic character for itself, "extended" in a discontinuous way by that of the animal, which is aleatory in the second degree as philosophy can be within this quantum perspective, man-in-person or the before-priority generic clone extends with the same rupture through the animal as a clone of simple priority. The clone is not a lesser human, but it is under-determined in a generic way, and this is a way of protecting it. The philosophical servitude of man is prolonged by that of the animals, the protection of the weakest and the struggle against philosophical sufficiency and the human-philosophers who carry it is a means of defending animals. The degrowth of philosophy or of the metaphysical nature of the animal-world is the condition for reaching the animal, for reaching its generic clone. The degrowth of the animal is not an ontological diminishing, an abasement and impoverishment, it is based on the opposition of the force of force, of the philosophical structure which serves as capital for eco-philosophers, and of the weak force of the generic with a simple priority, but which is dedicated to defense and not to domination.

These distinctions are directed against *the principle of Anthropic Sufficiency*, which is the implied content of its physico-natural formulation as an *anthropic principle that amounts to immediately or in-itself positing the anthropos*. To break this vicious essence linked to its syntax, which is the mark of positivity and philosophical spontaneity, and in order to denounce its naturalistic understanding, it suffices to cast doubt on this sufficiency with probability and randomness, not to mention with the complexity of the quantum apparatus, even as de-mathematized. There is a certain reciprocal determination between the generic man(-animal) and its knowledge, but this is only probable, an under-determination that in fact sets the relation within a non-relation.

A certain subtraction by the square root of -1 operates on the philosophical representation of the individual, meaning through vectors in a configuration space, generic man uses this apparatus to under-determine individuals as clones.

Man as Idempotence-in-Person or the In-the-Last-Humanity

We will not treat man, animal, and plant as identities in-themselves, we will not exchange them as if they were reversible, man participates in the animal, the plant and the man from whom he splits himself as a generic under-determining of the others and himself, but this will never be a strict equivalent, even with himself.

The three living beings will not be treated in the modality of a difference in general and an ontological difference in particular. The anthropo-logical distinction is not copied from ontological difference as irreversible, it is quantum, algebraic, and generic in nature.

Man will be treated as participating necessarily in the animal but not being exhausted there, such that man participates without being reducible to the animal. And we will treat the animal as necessarily having a human aspect, but not reducible to its simple naked representation of this aspect, which is also determined in-the-last-humanity. The generic must be understood as the same split instance, therefore in a relation of idempotence with itself. The difference between the three living things is that man is the bearer of the in-the-last-humanity and so responsible for its diffusion to and among the other living things who receive the generic in a simple state. Maybe the only human originality is in their power to split, which they exercise in the same generic function. This is precisely idempotence. Man is Idempotence-in-person, we can say nothing more or less, idempotence denying itself in order to diffuse itself in all living things.

AFTERWORD: QUANTUM LARUELLE – A PRINCIPLE OF PHILOSOPHICAL UNCERTAINTY

JOHN Ó MAOILEARCA

Christ, not an Afterword as well? Believe you me, I would much prefer not to. Besides, it would be all too easy to compose some kind of sub-Derridean, or just "Derridean," missive on the immanent illogic of the "after-word," or indeed, the fore-word too for that matter. Self-effacing gestures of the writer's impasse aside, nobody would want to read it either. Plus, I've already written at too great a length on the near impossibility of introducing Laruelle's work, so how on earth could I presume to give the *last* word on his work, or even at least this work, now? To attempt to determine his meaning after the fact, in the "last instance" – as Laruelle might write – would be all too much a vision-in-hindsight, a retrospective logic of the spirit of his word, if not its letter: mysticism over syntax. And, of course, clever-clogs that Laruelle is, he has anticipated this moment in any case: In his earlier book, *Philosophies of Difference*, he decries the habit of philosophers who are prone to somewhat artificially raising problems of doctrinal coherence in order to give oneself the function and the 'benefit' of resolving them. [. . .] 'There is an insurmountable contradiction: see how I know the author better than he himself, how I myself am a good author, more Kantian than Kant, more Spinozist than Spinoza![1]

What chance, then, to be more Laruellean than Laruelle with this last word, given Laruelle's auto-immunizing gesture? No doubt there are contradictions (real or apparent) to be unearthed in his non-philosophy, such as when he strives to be absolutely consistent with the logic of deconstruction when writing, or rather performing, his "post-deconstructionist" thoughts (as he himself has described them). More Derridean than Derrida himself, then? Perhaps we might be allowed to turn the tables on Laruelle too?

Certainly, there are many aspects to this book, *The Last Humanity*, that could motivate such a reversal. For instance, if there is a "Laruelle 101," its central, minimal, tenet is that thought is democratic, and standard philosophy is the gesture that creates hierarchy in thought. Non-philosophical practice, by contrast, endeavors to undo or flatten that hierarchy by de-authorizing philosophy's presumption of conceptual supremacy. So, what price then, *The Last Humanity* describing certain forms of ecological thought as "vulgar," or even "cynical"? Is Laruelle's objective to alienate even his most sympathetic readers? Surely, he has enough enemies already, both inside and outside the academy. In his defense, Laruelle has long derided what he calls the "spontaneous" philosophies that non-standard philosophical practices can import from (or have imposed by) standard philosophy: think only of those art theorists or practitioners who have used Heidegger or Deleuze as a conceptual crutch. For Laruelle, there is no need for an exterior authority (philosophy) to underpin art's conceptual innovations: the thought-forms native to such practices are of equal value to all others, being immanently relative to the Real. Remember, Laruelle is adopting a difference stance or posture, a quasi-physical reorientation of certain "habits" or *behaviors* (such as "being more X than X," mentioned earlier). There are many similar behaviors found among the philosophers: "founding, reducing, subtracting, withdrawing, suspecting, critiquing, anticipating/retarding, overthrowing, meditating, elucidating, analyzing, synthetizing, deconstructing and constructing, etc."[2] Might we add "afterwording"? And in *The Last Humanity*, Laruelle does indeed say (p.79) that "we are not doing exegesis or hermeneutics, we take them [philosophical formulas] up through their behavior, which is that of axioms that will serve as *variables* in this apparatus." This book, *The Last Humanity*, is that apparatus, one that adopts alternative behaviors, a form of movement or *variability* that attempts to reorient our more habitual inclinations.

This kind of vectorial thinking, thinking as movement, is not a form of structuralism, therefore, for the latter is far too unvarying. Non-philosophy is perpetually mutating in order *not to adopt a position – position equals authority* – and that is in part what makes it appear so perfidious to some. For now we come to what is most contentious about *The Last Humanity* – its apparent humanism. Again, there is nothing new in Laruelle placing the human as the center of his thought as a synonym for the Real. Yet it is no coincidence that the translator of *The Last Humanity*, Anthony Paul Smith, has himself produced a very Laruellean engagement with ecological thought, *A Non-Philosophical Theory of Nature*.[3] Nor is it a mere accident that one of Laruelle's first significant interpreters, Katerina Kolozova, has produced two books using Laruelle's non-philosophy to engage in a non-anthropocentric vision of the animal and nonhuman.[4] And even my own *All Thoughts Are Equal* sought to invent a nonhuman philosophy using animal models without any deference to the human, all while adopting a Laruellean posture. Now, in the face of Laruelle's latest work and its hierarchy between "vulgar" ecologism (so much for the value of the "ordinary," one might add) and Laruelle's "new ecological science," as well as its perpetuation of a (philosophical) dualism between man and nature (albeit with much added non-standard subtlety), one might well pose the question: are we, Laruelle's interpreters, all suffering from "hallucinations" (to use Laruelle's term), or are we simply idiots?

Hopefully, not. Take a section from the book such as the following:

> this ethico-ecological comportment is not a decision or an event
> but an opaque or probable process. But can ethics be probable
> instead of dogmatic, as it naturally tends to be? If there is a higher
> ethics, a supreme principle for ethical rules themselves, it amounts
> to protecting human living beings as 'in-the-last-humanity' or as a
> power to under-determine rationalist ethics and other sorts that are
> all based upon philosophical sufficiency (p.138)

The ethics that puts the human at its center is not a decision—which
would make it a philosophical position—but a process, one modeled
on quantum probability. God—if He existed—*would* play dice. Such a
process humanism might remind one of Bergson's in *The Two Sources
of Morality and Religion*, which appears to espouse an "anthropic
principle" almost as radical as Laruelle's here, only for it to be rendered
processual on account of the "human" only being a placeholder for a
moral form (pure openness) that any other animal might have fulfilled
in an alternative universe. The human has no other essence than
openness, which is itself *not to have an essence* (it is a process ethics
after all). And Laruelle echoes this point (such that we would have to
dub Bergson a non-philosopher *avant la lettre*): "only man can possess
this algebraic system, it is not an essence for all eternity but an
operative process, a minimal logos, the minimum necessary calculation
or possible language and not a sufficient or essential account" (p104).
And this minimalism is crucial, because, while it is of course true
that Laruelle never falls into "vulgar" philosophical anthropology—
philosophies *of* or *about* the human that actually "harass" the human
with exclusive and exclusionary properties via Aristotle, Descartes,
Hegel, Nietzsche, Heidegger, etc.—it is equally certain that he does
not say who the humans are that he equates with this minimal essence
or definition. The human, like the animal, and the plant, are always
placeholders within a system or network ('MAP', as he calls it). That is
the rule of the quantum.

It is noteworthy in this regard that the earlier incarnation of Laruelle's ideas in Non-Philosophy II also conveyed an apparent contradiction by replacing philosophy for science at the center of thought: was not this scientism simply an all-too philosophical reversal (that could easily be itself reversed later) when what we were promised was a true non-hierarchy, a flat thought? No, the contradiction is only apparent because the substitution was never of "centers" anyway. As Laruelle wrote at the time: "when science is really 'at the centre,' there is no longer center or periphery. Nothing, not even philosophy, turns around it."[5] Pure openness. And, in the guise of Laruelle's most recent Non-Philosophy V, effective since 2008 with the quantum-turn in his thought, it is not that quantum mechanics is the positive science to which everything must be reduced. Rather, it is the model of uncertainty, indeterminacy, and processuality through which we can rethink everything, *in the last instance*. And this is what the human is too, even in *The Last Humanity*. What or who the human is, is foreclosed to thought, just as the Real is. The Human is a model, a placeholder, a minimal form of radical openness. Which is also to say that when we think alongside Laruelle, rather than about him, we should, in the last instance, follow the quantum model and make him, and our words, uncertain. If this last word appears to be making Laruelle *more* Laruellean then, it is only by following a minimalist principle, an insufficient quantum of Laruelle.

Notes

Translator's Introduction: Why Ecology at the End

1 François Laruelle and Philippe Petit, *Intellectuals and Power: The Insurrection of the Victim*, trans. Anthony Paul Smith (Cambridge: Polity, 2014), p. 15.

2 See Christian Lévêque, *Ecology: From Ecosystem to Biosphere* (Plymouth, UK: Science Publisher, Inc., 2003), pp. v–vi, 3–4, 8–9.

3 Aldo Leopold, "The Land Ethic" in *A Sand Country Almanac* (Oxford: Oxford University Press, 1968), pp. 202–03.

4 Leopold, p. 204.

5 Environmental historians have been at the forefront of uncovering and exploring this aspect of ecology. Some classics of this genre include Alfred W. Crosby, *Ecological Imperialism: The Biological Expansion of Europe, 900-1900* (Cambridge: Cambridge University Press, 1986), William Cronin, *Changes in the Land: Indians, Colonists, and the Ecology of New England* (New York: Hill & Wang, 2003), William Cronin, *Nature's Metropolis: Chicago and the Great West* (New York: W.W. Norton, 1991), and Donald Worster, *Nature's Economy: A History of Ecological Ideas* (Cambridge: Cambridge University Press, 1994).

6 See Frank B. Golley, *A History of the Ecosystem Concept in Ecology: More Than the Sum of the Parts* (New Haven: Yale University Press, 1993), pp. 8–34. Pedar Ankar argues that these debates were part and parcel of debates about the social, economic, and ecological management of colonies in Anker, *Imperial Ecology: Environmental Order in the British Empire, 1895-1945* (Cambridge, MA: Harvard University Press, 2002).

7 Readers interested in a more direct non-philosophical engagement with the scientific concepts and practices of ecology are invited to see my own work on this topic. In *A Non-Philosophical Theory of Nature: Ecologies of Thought* (New York: PalgraveMacmillian, 2013) I develop a unified theory of philosophical theology and scientific ecology to consider anew the concept of nature. There you will find non-philosophical mutations of major ecological concepts like ecosystem, biodiversity, and the niche.

8 Here the grammar in which our thinking is unable to express this thought clearly and so the relational element required by our grammar, the preposition "to," is suspended to better express the nature of radical immanence.

9 François Laruelle, "Non-Philosophy, Weapon of Last Defense" in *Laruelle and Non-Philosophy*, eds. John Ó Maoilearca and Anthony Paul Smith (Edinburgh: Edinburgh University Press, 2012), p. 241.

10 Laruelle does this with non-philosophy too. See his *Struggle and Utopia at the End Times of Philosophy*, trans. Drew S. Burk and Anthony Paul Smith (Minneapolis: Univocal Publishing, 2013) where he criticizes certain seeds of authority-based thinking in non-philosophy.

11 To date Katerina Kolozova has given the most thought to questions of gender using non-philosophy. See Kolozova, *The Cut of the Real: Subjectivity in Poststructuralist Philosophy* (New York: Columbia University Press, 2014). Given the lack of work in this area it is clear that questions related to gender, sexuality, and queerness still challenge non-philosophy and that this work remains to be done.

12 See Sylvia Wynter, "Unsettling the Coloniality of Being/Power/Truth/ Freedom: Towards the Human, After Man, Its Overrepresentation—An Argument" in *CR: The New Centennial Review* 3.3 (Fall 2003): pp. 257–337. The essays in *Sylvia Wyter: On Being Human as Praxis*, ed. Katherine McKittrick (Durham: Duke University Press, 2015) also provide useful material for any future possible conversation between the work of Laruelle and Wynter.

13 See the popular work of the Out of the Woods Collective, especially "Refugees and Death-Worlds" and "Infrastructure Against Borders" available online at https://libcom.org/blog/refuges-death-worlds-25112016 and https://libcom.org/blog/infrastructure-against-borders-06122016.

Forword

1 *Vectoriell* translated the French *vectorial* as a distinct word from *vectoriel* (which translates to the English "vectorial" and refers to the normal mathematical sense). Laruelle is here calling upon Heidegger's distinction between *existenziell* and *existenzial*. Following other recent translations of Laruelle I have marked this echo of Heidegger by echoing the English translation of *existenziell* as *existnentiell*. Readers should note that the normal French word *vectoriel* does not appear in this text. Readers may notice other variations of this as well.—Translator's note.

2 The French *l'en-dernière-humanité* takes a grammatical form similar to *l'en-soi* or "the in-itself" and so I have translated it as "the in-the-last-humanity." — Translator's note.

Introduction

1 Crossroads here translates the French *carrefour*, which is the usual French translation of Heidegger's concept of *das Geivert*, known in English as "the fourfold." Given the coordinates Laruelle is working within here, the reference seems clear though occluded when moving from German to French to English.—Translator's note.

2 This reference is to Irenaeus who writes: "The glory of God is a living man; and the life of man consists in beholding God" (*Against Heresies*, Book 4, 20:7).—Translator's note.

Chapter 1 In Search of a Messianic Ecology

1 The adjective "physical" should be read as referring to quantum physics and not to physical in the more mundane sense.—Translator's note.

Chapter 3 The House of Philosophy Is in Ruins

1   I have translated quantique as "the quantum" throughout this text, while the French can also be translated as "quantum physics," Laruelle uses the term quantique to refer to something more expansive like "quantum thought" or "quantum science" which quantum physics is a part of.— Translator's note.

Afterword

1   François Laruelle, "Controversy over the Possibility of a Science of Philosophy," in François Laruelle, *Non-Philosophy Project: Essays by François Laruelle*. Edited by Gabriel Alkon and Boris Gunjevic (New York: Telos, 2012), pp.74–92: p.88.

2   François Laruelle, *Anti-Badiou: On the Introduction of Maoism into Philosophy* (London: Bloomsbury, 2013), pp.212–13. Italics mine.

3   Anthony Paul Smith, *A Non-Philosophical Theory of Nature: Ecologies of Thought* (Basingstoke: Palgrave Macmillan, 2013).

4   Katerina Kolozava, *The Lived Revolution: Solidarity with the Body in Pain as the New Political Universal* (Skopje, Macedonia: Evro-Balkan Press, 2010); Katerina Kolozava, *Capitalism's Holocaust of Animals* (London: Bloomsbury, 2019).

5   See Taylor Adkins, "Death of the Translator, a Uni-lateral Odyssey." In François Laruelle, *Philosophy and Non-Philosophy*, Translated by Taylor Adkins (Minneapolis, Minnesota: Univocal, 2013), vi.

Index